FIRST TIMOTHY 2:12

WHAT DOES THE BIBLE REALLY SAY ABOUT WOMEN PASTORS/PREACHERS?

EDWARD D. ANDREWS

FIRST TIMOTHY 2:12

What Does the Bible Really Say About Women Pastors/Preachers?

Edward D. Andrews

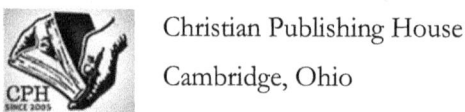

Christian Publishing House

Cambridge, Ohio

Copyright © 2019 Edward D. Andrews

All rights reserved. Except for brief quotations in articles, other publications, book reviews, and blogs, no part of this book may be reproduced in any manner without prior written permission from the publishers. For information, write, support@christianpublishers.org

Unless otherwise stated, Scripture quotations are from the Updated American Standard Version (UASV) by Christian Publishing House

FIRST TIMOTHY 2:12: What Does the Bible Really Say About Women Pastors/Preachers? by Edward D. Andrews

ISBN-13: **978-1-949586-94-7**

ISBN-10: **1-949586-94-4**

For All the Women

Table of Contents

INTRODUCTION WOMEN IN THE PULPIT? 7
BIBLICAL VIEWPOINT 8

CHAPTER 1 FIRST TIMOTHY 2:9-15 WHAT DOES THE BIBLE REALLY SAY ABOUT WOMEN PASTORS/PREACHERS? 13
INSTRUCTIONS FOR WOMEN....................................15
SPIRITUAL LEADERSHIP 17
IN SILENCE..18
WITH ALL SUBMISSIVENESS 19
BUT TO BE IN QUIETNESS 24
2:12 GREEK, GRAMMAR & SYNTAX...........................25
HEAD COVERING EXCURSION 31
2:13 GREEK, GRAMMAR & SYNTAX...........................33
GENESIS 3:6 EXCURSION..36
BUT THE WOMAN WAS DECEIVED..............................41
AND CAME TO BE IN TRANSGRESSION 42
2:14 GREEK, GRAMMAR & SYNTAX...........................43
WHAT ABOUT ROMANS 16:7? 48
WHAT ABOUT THE ARGUMENT THAT PAUL WROTE THOSE THINGS BECAUSE HE LIVED IN A PATRIARCHAL SOCIETY OR CULTURE THAT INFLUENCED HIM? 49
WAS DEBORAH A RULER OF ANCIENT ISRAEL? 49
WHAT ABOUT THE WOMEN WHO CLAIM THAT THEY ARE CALLED TO PASTOR A CHURCH? THE WOMEN SAY, 'IT IS OUR CALLING? WHO ARE YOU TO REJECT A PERSON CALLED BY GOD?' 51
WHAT DID THE APOSTLE PAUL MEAN WOMEN TO KEEP SILENT IN THE CONGREGATIONS? ARE THE WOMEN NOT TO SPEAK AT ALL?..52

CHAPTER 2 WAS THE APOSTLE PAUL AGAINST WOMEN? 54

- CONTEXT OF 1 TIMOTHY 2:12-13 54
- PAUL THE APOSTLE 63
- THE WOMEN OF PAUL'S LETTERS 63
- DID PAUL EVIDENCE ANTI-FEMALE BIAS? 64
- "WOMAN ... TO BE IN SILENCE" 65
- FULL SUBMISSIVENESS 68

CHAPTER 3 GENDER-INCLUSIVE LANGUAGE IN BIBLE TRANSLATION 70

- THE CHIEF TRANSLATION PRINCIPLE IS ACCURACY 72

CHAPTER 4 WHAT DOES WIFELY SUBJECTION MEAN? 81

- DISCERNMENT NEEDED 82
- THE HUSBAND WHO IGNORES HIS HEADSHIP 83

CHAPTER 5 WHAT DOES SUBJECTION IN MARRIAGE MEAN? 85

- SUBJECTION IS RELATIVE 93

OTHER BOOK BY ANDREWS 105

BIBLIOGRAPHY 109

INTRODUCTION Women in the Pulpit?

This very brief introduction will acquaint the reader with the issue at hand. Today, many women in the Christian feminist movement see the discussion of this subject by a male author as being pro-patriarchy, complementarian, and that we believe women should be kept entirely silent in church. This simply is not the case for an author like Andrews, who is always after the truth no matter where it leads. It might be useful to begin by defining some terms from a feminist perspective. The truth of God's Word, the Bible, is far from the dominant, patriarchal oppressive, and exploitive caricature that modern Christian feminism distorts in their exaggerated feminist theology.

Christian feminism is a school of Christian theology that seeks to advance and understand the equality of men and women morally, socially, spiritually, and in leadership from a Christian perspective.[1]

Complementarianism is a theological view in Christianity, Judaism, and Islam that men and women have different but complementary roles and responsibilities.

Feminist theology is a movement found in several religions, including Buddhism, Christianity, Judaism, and New Thought, to reconsider the traditions, practices, scriptures, and theologies of those religions from a **feminist** perspective.

Patriarchy as a system of social structures and practices in which men dominate, oppress, and exploit **women**."

Womanist theology is a religious conceptual framework that reconsiders and revises the traditions, practices, scriptures, and biblical interpretation with a unique lens to empower and liberate African American women in America.

In the past 30-50 years, many Protestant denominations have altered their church policy to ordain female pastors, ministers, and preachers. Among these are Lutherans, Episcopalians, Anglicans,

---

[1] Hassey, Janette (1989). "A Brief History of Christian Feminism". Transformation. 6 (2): 1–5. doi:10.1177/026537888900600201. JSTOR 43052265

American Baptist Church,[2] Presbyterian Church, United Church of Christ, United Methodist Church, Pentecostal Church of God, and Assemblies of God, to mention a few. We should note that many Catholic activists have argued for the ordaining of women for decades.

After 2,000 years of only men serving as priests, pastors, and ministers, we might ask why we are now seeing this push to ordain women. It is merely a product of the modern-day liberation movement of women. Christian feminists and female theologians have long contended from their interpretation of Scripture that women are equally qualified "to teach or exercise authority over" the Christian congregation. While the Christian feminists and female theologians are seeking to "abolish tradition," it is best to ask to whom God has given this responsibility of teaching the Christian congregation. In this short but biblically sound publication, we will exegetically investigate the Bible's view.

Biblical Viewpoint

Unlike the Pharisees and Jewish religious leaders, Jesus showed much love for women, as he treated them with respect and readily taught them. Women loyally assisted Jesus and were the first to see Jesus after his resurrection, serving as a witness, which was unheard of for females to be witnesses at this time. – John 4:27; Luke 10:39; Matt. 27:55, 56; 28:1, 9.

There is not one verse in the four Gospels that would suggest that Jesus ever discouraged his female disciples from proclaiming the "good news" of salvation. In fact, after the outpouring of the Holy Spirit at Pentecost upon the 120 men and *women* assembled, Peter quoted the prophecy of Joel. "'And in the last days it shall be, God declares, that I will pour out my Spirit on all flesh, and your sons and your *daughters* shall prophesy ...'" (Acts 1:14; 2:1-18; Joel 2:28, 29) Thus, we can see that in the early Christian congregation both men and women were very eager to share the good news of the kingdom with any who might listen.

However, we have to dig deeper into the use of the Greek word *diakonos*. It can be rendered as a "servant" or "minister," that is, either a male or female "serving" or "ministering to," attending to the needs of another. Paul uses it in this way when he is speaking of "Phoebe, a servant

---

[2] It should be noted that there are some 66+ different Baptist denominations.

[*diakonon*]of the church at Cenchreae." (Rom. 16:1; Luke 8:1-3) In many passages, however, the word specifically refers to an appointed person in the church, which is rendered deacon by all literal translations except the forthcoming Updated American Standard Version (UASV),[3] where it is rendered "servant." Note that this verse is shortly after our upcoming discussion of 1 Timothy 2:8-15.

If we look at the list of qualifications for the position of "deacon" or "servant," it includes being "the husband of one wife." The same is said of the "elder," "overseer," "pastor." The "pastor" must be "a **man** who manages **his** own household well, having his children in subjection[4] with all seriousness." (1 Tim. 3:2-4, 8, 12) So, it is the baptized men members of the church who are eligible to hold leadership positions (pastor and deacon).

The Greek New Testament is evident on this matter. The apostle Paul writes: "I do not permit a woman to teach [the church] or to exercise authority over a man … (1 Tim. 2:11-12) Yet, elsewhere, Paul does speak of women having the ability to teach, for he encourages mature women to be "teaching what is good, so that they may encourage the young women." (Titus 2:3-5) Why is it that women can teach other women but cannot teach the men? Was the apostle Paul some **patriarchal** man who dominated, oppressed, and exploited **women**." Was Paul "antiwoman"?

This modern-day feminist mindset tries to impose its way of thinking while ignoring the fundamental teachings of the Bible: headship. The apostle Paul was in harmony with the apostle Peter and other New Testament authors when he wrote, "But I want you to understand that the head of every man is Christ, the head of a wife is her husband, and the head of Christ is God." – 1 Corinthians 11:3; 1 Peter 3:1.

The only person without any headship is the Father; all others do have a headship. This provision of headship is actually beneficial for all. God offered the family balance for life's most intimate relationships. Just as you have one president of a country, one captain on a ship, one head pastor in a church, you have one family member who takes the lead, giving direction. God gave this responsibility to man. He also commanded, "the husbands should love their wives as their own bodies. He who loves his wife loves himself. For no one ever hated his own flesh, but nourishes and cherishes it, just as Christ does the church … let each

---

[3] https://www.uasvbible.org/

[4] Or *keep children under control*

one of you love his wife as himself, and let the wife see that she respects her husband." – Ephesians 5:28-33.

Therefore, if the woman must seek the husband's guidance and direction in the home, how would it be possible for her to take her husband's headship and other men and women in the church? What would the situation be like if you had a male and female pastor and they were married to each other?

The modern-day feminist who advocated for female pastors says that it was the day's social custom that prevented Jesus from choosing a female apostle among the twelve. However, this is a non-started, as God and his Son, Jesus Christ, are not motivated by social customs. Otherwise, Jesus would never have taught the women, or Paul would have never allowed the women to be taught or allowed them to be used in special ways to assist the ministry. Jesus acted in harmony with God's Word, God's original purpose. In the Garden of Eden, Adam, the man, was Eve, the woman's head, even before the fall into sin. – Genesis 2:18, 22, 24; 1 Corinthians 11:7-9.

Is the way God has chosen to use men and women to carry out His will and purposes somehow impeding women? Does this somehow make the women of the church "second-class Christians," as some feminists have claimed? The word "submission" has a negative connotation today, with the sense of "inferiority." However, we do not evaluate the Word of God based on the whims of changing cultures and uses of terminology. God is outside of time and culture. If we adopted different cultures worldwide in our interpreting process, we would have hundreds of different meanings throughout the past 2,000 years. Both men and women are in "submission" to God, seeking to do his will as he sees fit because he sees the big picture. If we do not bulk at that will, we will find happiness.

Many times, because the modern-day interpreter wishes to read their feelings into the text, the apostle Paul is often misrepresented concerning women. The apostle Paul wrote extensively on how women should be loved and respected; he frequently greeted and commended by name the individual sisters who played a role in his life and ministry. (Rom. 16:3, 4, 6, 12) Moreover, Paul wrote the verse in Galatians 3:28, which is most often quoted by advocates of women pastors, ministers, and priests. "There is neither Jew nor Greek, there is neither slave nor free man, there is *neither male nor female*; for you are all one in Christ Jesus." (Italics mine)

This verse's context reveals that it is not referring to who can take the lead in the church, but Paul is now referring to being one in Christ.

Under Judaism, women were viewed with disdain, seen as less in their being part of God's people because they could not be circumcised. Here Paul is saying that anyone can be a disciple of Christ regardless of their ethnic group, their station in life, or their gender. However, they must come to Christ in the same way, through faith and repentance. When we remove the distinctions, we are all one in Christ. This does not mean that the roles that we are assigned by God are erased.

male nor female,

Ancient society, including the Jews, usually took a disparaging view of women. Since women could not receive circumcision, they were less than full participants in the old covenant. The Talmud (the official collection of Jewish tradition and Scripture interpretation) has some very harsh statements in this regard: "Women are greedy, inquisitive, lazy, vain, and frivolous";[5] "Ten *qab* of empty-headedness have come upon the world,[6] nine having been received by women, and one by the rest of the world"; "Happy is he whose children are males, and woe to him whose children are females."[7] Worst of all, the rabbis taught, "May the words of the Torah be burned, they should not be handed over to women."[8]

But in Christ women come to faith (v. 26), baptism (v. 27), and salvation (v. 29) on the same terms with men. They are equally acceptable to God, and equally loved.

This does not, however, cancel out the separate and distinct roles of men and women in the home or in the church.[9] It was after Paul had written this verse in

---

[5] bShab 33b.

[6] bQid 49b.

[7] bQid 82b.

[8] jSota 18d, 8.

[9] Fung, p. 176, esp. n. 44.

> Galatians that he affirmed certain limitations on the role of women (1 Cor 11:3–16; 14:33–36; 1 Tim 2:8–15). The statement "neither male nor female" must be understood in terms of eligibility for salvation, especially in this context of faith and baptism (vv. 26–27).
>
> On the other hand, others hold that this verse removes virtually all distinctions between men and women in the church. Bruce reasons that "if a Gentile may exercise spiritual leadership in church as freely as a Jew, or a slave as freely as a citizen, why not a woman as freely as a man?"[10] While slave/master roles would still exist between Christians outside the context of the church, and while husband/wife roles would still exist in the family, no such distinctions would be recognized in their church roles. However, this is not implied by the context, and is inconsistent with Paul's own later teaching.[11]

Thus, while all of the different denominations and churches are split on this issue, Christian women are best served by being obedient to the Word of God, as opposed to the shifting winds of what Satan's world of fallen humanity think, feel, and believe. In being faithful to God, there is no being repressed. The genuine Christian woman finds true happiness in serving God within the confines of his Word. (1 Pet. 2:5) They can teach women and children within the church in Bible study classes. They can play different parts on the stage before main services (singing, dramas, etc.). They can teach and make disciples outside of the church. (Matt. 24:14; 28:19-20; Ac 1:8) They can be Christian authors.

---

[10] Bruce, p. 190. Fung (p. 176) notes that unlike the Jew/Gentile and slave/free distinctions, the male/female distinction has its roots in creation.

[11] Kenneth L. Boles, *Galatians & Ephesians*, The College Press NIV Commentary (Joplin, MO: College Press, 1993), Ga 3:28.

CHAPTER 1 First Timothy 2:9-15 What Does the Bible Really Say About Women Pastors/Preachers?

What modern-day Christians fail to understand is this: to deviate, in any way, from the pattern, or likeness of how God brought his Word into existence, merely opens the Bible up to a book that reflects the age and time of its readers. If we allow the Bible to be altered because the progressive woman's movement feels offended by masculine language, the condemnation of homosexuality, the husband as the head of the family, and forbidding the woman to teach the church, it will not be long before the Bible gives way to the homosexual communities being offended by God's Words in the book of Romans; so modern translations will then tame that language, to not offend. I am confident that we thought that we would never see the day of two men or two women being married by priests, but that day has been upon us for some time now. In fact, the American government is debating whether to change the definition of marriage. Moreover, we now are doing away with gender in American society. Therefore, I would suggest that the liberal readers do not take my warning here as radicalism, but more as reality.

When we look at the controversy over gender-inclusive language (more on this later) and the use of plurals, the above principles come into play, as does the historical-grammatical approach, which means that God personally chose the time, the place, the language, and the culture into which his Word was inspirationally penned. Who are we to disrespect that because we wish to appease the modern man or woman, who may be offended? Their offense is nothing more than self-centeredness, refusing to wrap their mind around the idea that the Creator of all things chose the setting, the language, and time in which his Word was to be introduced to man.

1 Timothy 2:12 Updated American Standard Version (UASV)

12 I do not permit a woman to teach or to exercise authority over a man; rather, she is to remain quiet.

Before beginning, let us note that this is not to say that a female cannot carry out the great commission, which requires teaching in other capacities within the church and outside the church. The female Christian can teach Bible study to young children (not baptized young men), or young women, or adult women within the church. The female can proclaim the good news to and teach unbelievers. These things are not in opposition to what the apostle Paul under inspiration penned on this subject and are permissible.

This chapter will be a careful discussion of the correct interpretation of 1 Timothy 2:9-15. Specifically, we will focus on 1 Timothy 2:12, where Paul's natural reading is understood as instructing Timothy that women are not to teach or have authority over men in the Christian congregation.

There is little doubt as to why there are different conclusions about the meaning of 1 Timothy 2:12. **(1)** The interpreter does not follow grammatical-historical principles of interpretation but rather grammatical-critical-historical principles of interpretation. **(2)** In addition, the interpreter takes the passage out of context. **(3)** Moreover, the interpreter misinterprets historical-cultural background. **(4)** Furthermore, little or incorrect attention is given to lexical or grammatical matters.

Instructions for Women

1 Timothy 2:9-10 Updated American Standard Version (UASV)

⁹ Likewise, women are to adorn themselves with appropriate clothing, with modesty and soundness of mind,[12] not with braided hair and gold or pearls or costly garments, ¹⁰ but with what is proper for women professing godly reverence, by means of good works.

Paul discussed how women should dress and carry themselves in times of public worship and public prayer. In the days of the apostles, it was a custom among women in that world of Greek culture to go in for extravagant hairstyles and other adornments. While it is true that Paul was literally talking about how a woman should "dress," yet his overall point was not only that she should dress modestly but that the adornment is not merely external but is also internal in how she carries herself and her attitude and obligations toward God.

The "dress" "modestly" means that a woman is to dress discerningly (tastefully) and not provocatively. The Greek term rendered "dress" (*katastolē*) has the sense of an outward deportment, how the woman behaves, carries, and presents herself, especially when it comes to dressing, especially in worship. This goes beyond merely dressing sensually; it also applies to her not flaunting her wealth either. Paul is suggesting a neatness and good, pleasing appearance, not calling attention to one's wealth or beauty. The Christian woman's manner of dressing should not be shocking to the Christians' moral susceptibilities within the congregation, offending some.

---

[12] Or *good sense; discreetness*

The apostle Paul encouraged the women to focus their attention on "good works" instead of their physical appearance. Some men in the Christian congregation had "the appearance of godliness." (2 Tim. 3:5) Not only did these wicked men seek to corrupt their fellow Christians through false teachings, but they also sought to involve the women of the congregation in sexually immoral conduct. As the disciple Jude noted: "Certain men have crept in among you who were long ago appointed for this judgment, ungodly men[13] who change[14] the grace of our God into an excuse for licentiousness[15] and who prove false to our only Master and Lord, Jesus Christ." Some of the women in Ephesus sought to fulfill their sexual urges by taking advantage of these wicked men's motives, doing so by coming to church seductively dressed.

Second Timothy 3:6 indicates that these false teachers focused their attention primarily on "**weak women**." This reference to "weak women" (Gr. *gunaikaria*) here is not the same as the "weaker vessel" (Gr. *asthenestero skeuei*) referred to at 1 Peter 3:7. Instead, "weak women" refers to being spiritually or morally weak "women weighed down with sins, led on by various desires," as is indicated by the context. These ungodly men, these false teachers, did not openly make advance their views and desires but rather 'those men] who crept into (slyly, secretively entering, worming one's way into) households. Mind you, this is not

---

[13] Lit *irreverential (ones)*

[14] Or *turn*

[15] Or loose conduct; shameless conduct (Gr *aselgeia*) behavior completely lacking in moral restraint, usually with the implication of sexual licentiousness, – 'licentious behavior, extreme immorality.'

single women but married women. Once these ungodly men have worked their way into the bed of spiritually or morally weak married women, they seek to influence the entire household through the woman. These women were not well-grounded in the Word of God, so they readily surrender to false teachers who, possibly by a graceful manner and flattering speech, make it seem as though they are apostles of righteousness.

These "weak women **weighed down with sins**, led on by **various desires**" had sinful inclinations, and their desires weighed heavily upon them. It isn't as though they genuinely hated what was bad and loved righteousness. The ungodly men, false teachers, preyed on such weaknesses. These men convinced the spiritually weak women to immoral sexual relations based on a twisted view that God understands human weaknesses, so they would be easily forgiven because God is merciful. The apostle Paul warned against these desires and called on the women to focus on good works. It should be noted that there are many spiritually strong women, as is true of men too, who learn the truths within God's Word, and they hold onto it.

Spiritual Leadership

1 Timothy 2:11 Updated American Standard Version (UASV)

[11] Let a woman learn in silence with all submissiveness.

11 Let a woman

Woman (Gr., *gunē*), as it is used here in the singular, means women in general, not just wives,[16] as it has throughout this section of text (8-15). In verse 9, Paul addresses how women are to carry themselves, namely, their dress and outward appearance. In verse 10, Paul speaks of what is proper for women, who profess godliness, which is that they should be helpful to others; in other words, good works.

learn (let her be learning) **(Why and How?)**[17]

As an inspired author, the apostle Paul had actually extended to women more consideration than they ever had in Judaism. Having the privilege and right to Learn (Gr., *manthaneto*), outside of the home was not something Jewish women of the first century would have ever considered. Paul was not borrowing from Judaism of the time, who also did not allow women to speak, having to remain silent. Judaism could care less about women growing in knowledge of God's Word. On the other hand, Paul had said explicitly that they were to learn in silence, knowing that they were ministers of the good news as well, just not in the church, over the congregation of men, baptized brothers. 1 Corinthians 14:34; Genesis 2:18–25; 3:16

In silence

In silence (Gr., *hesuchia*) meant that the woman was 'to be quietness,' 'to be still.' In other words, she was to show respect for her head, man, especially the congregation's leadership by not raising questions, attempting to teach.

---

[16] R. C. H. Lenski, The Interpretation of St. Paul's Epistles to the Colossians, to the Thessalonians, to Timothy, to Titus, and to Philemon (Columbus, Oh.: Wartburg, 1946), 562.

[17] In quietness, with all submissiveness

This was not a life of silence, just at the Christian congregation meetings. They were quietly to receive instruction at the meetings and ask their husbands questions in the privacy of their home. Thus, in the public meeting, the woman was to learn by listening, not teaching through questions. – 1 Corinthians 14:34-35.

with all submissiveness

Submissiveness (Gr., *hupotage*) means to be in "subjection, subordination, or submission," which is not being used in a negative sense. (2 Cor. 9:13; Gal. 2:5; 1 Tim. 2:11; 3:4) All Christians are to be submissive or in subjection to the Father, the Son, and superior authorities, which in no way detract from their human equality to each other, male or female. In the same sense, women are to be submissive to their husbands, man in general, and the men taking the lead in the Christian congregation.[18]

Here in verse 11, submissiveness refers to the relationship between women and men, especially men who hold a position of authority in the Christian congregation. Paul is very concerned that his words not be taken lightly, which is stressed by his addition of "in all or in entire (NASB) or in full (NIV) submissiveness." (See 1 Tim. 4:9; 5:2) While Paul is informing the Christian congregations that women are to take in as much knowledge about God and his Word as any man, this is not a means to their usurping man's position or authority within the congregation. In other words, the "all" is Paul stating emphatically that a woman's learning is not to be a pathway, to the role of authority over man, by way of teaching him.

---

[18] (1 Cor. 14:34; Eph. 5:21-22, 24; Col. 3:18; 1 Pet. 3:1, 5; Heb. 12:9; Jas. 4:7; 1 Cor. 16:16; 1 Pet. 5:5; Rom. 13:1, 5; 1 Tim. 3:4; Tit. 2:9; 3:1; 1 Pet. 2:18; Tit. 2:5; 1 Cor. 11:3, 4, 5, 7, 10; Eph. 5:23)

(See 1 Cor. 14:33-34) Yes, women are to learn in the Christian meetings, but it is being qualified in that it is to be (1) in silence and (2) in all submissiveness. Again, this subjection is to a position of authority, not as to person, as though women were/are inferior. Just as man is in subjection to Christ as their head, so is the woman to man, especially the husband.

1 Timothy 2:12 Updated American Standard Version (UASV)

¹² But I do not permit a woman to teach or to exercise authority over a man, but to be in quietness.

12 But I do not permit

But (de), could be rendered "but," "and, "so," "rather," among other things. This Greek conjunction de (used to link sentences, clauses, phrases, or words) could be used to simply connect the previous verse ("and"); however, it is best to take it as a contrast here. Verse 11 says what a woman **can do**, namely learn, although the learning is qualified as to how. Now, in verse 12, in contrast, a marked difference, Paul is stating what a woman **cannot do**. The woman may learn but may not teach or have authority over a man.

> If this were a descriptive present (as it is sometimes popularly taken), the idea might be that in the future the author would allow this: I do not presently permit… However, there are several arguments against this: (1) It is overly subtle. Without some temporal indicator, such as ἄρτι or perhaps νῦν, this view begs the question. (2) Were we to do this with other commands in the present tense, our resultant exegesis would be both capricious and ludicrous. Does μὴ μεθύσκεσθε οἴνῳ…, ἀλλὰ πληροῦσθε ἐν

πνεύματι in Eph. 5:18 mean "Do not for the moment be filled with wine, but be filled at the present time by the Spirit" with the implication that such a moral code might change in the future? The normal use of the present tense in didactic literature, especially when introducing an exhortation, is not descriptive, but a general precept that has gnomic[19] implications. (3) Grammatically, the present tense is used with a generic object (γυναικί), suggesting that it should be taken as a gnomic present. (4) Contextually, the exhortation seems to be rooted in creation (note v 13 and the introductory γάρ), rather than an address to a temporary situation.[20]

"I do not permit" is not Paul's personal opinion of things; this authority is in reference to Paul's being an apostolic author, who conveys the words of God, and not that he is making some personal rule because he fancies it, but that this has been the case since creation. (vs. 13), In 1 Corinthians 14:34, Paul gives us the same prohibition based on the law, "the women should keep silent in the churches. For they are not permitted to speak, but should be in submission, as the Law also says." (Gen. 3:16) There, same subject matter, in verse 37, Paul tells us where he gets that authority by stating, "The things I am writing to you are a command of the Lord." When it comes to 1 Timothy 2:11-12, and women not being permitted to teach, is this only applicable to the Ephesian and Corinthian Congregations or

---

[19] Gnomic: containing proverbs or other short pithy sayings that express basic truths

[20] Daniel B. Wallace, Greek Grammar Beyond the Basics – Exegetical Syntax of the New Testament, 525 (Zondervan Publishing House and Galaxie Software, 1999).

the first-century culture? George W. Knight addresses this partially in his commentary on 1 Timothy.

> It has also been suggested that the present indicative form of [epitrepo, "permitting"] indicates a temporal limitation and thus limits Paul's statement to the then and there of Ephesus. An examination of other occurrences of Paul's use of first person singular present indicative (Rom. 12:1, 3; 1 Cor. 4:16; 2 Cor. 5:20; Gal. 5:2-3, Eph. 4:1; 1 Thes. 4:1; 5:14; 2 Thes. 3:6; 1 Tim. 2:1, 8) demonstrates that he uses it to give universal and authoritative instruction or exhortation (cf. especially Rom. 12:1; 1 Tim. 2:8).[21]

a woman to teach[22] (Why / in what sense?)

As is true in verses 9 and 11, "woman" (γυνή, gune) is a reference to all women, women as a whole, which is underscored by the anarthrous (without the definite article) forms for both γυνή (a woman) and ἀνήρ (a man). In verse 11, it was women as a whole that was required to remain silent, and here it is women as a whole that is to refrain from teaching or exercising authority over a man.

These two verses are drawing an ever-increasing amount of comment today, but Paul's injunctions in 1 Timothy 2:11–12 require no special historical insights to understand. He says that women are not called to serve in the office of teacher or elder in the church. A crucial distinction to understand here is that between special and

---

[21] George W. Knight, The Pastoral Epistles: A Commentary on the Greek Text, New International Greek Testament Commentary, 140 (Grand Rapids, MI; Carlisle, England: W.B. Eerdmans; Paternoster Press, 1992).

[22] First qualifier as to "in silence"

general office ministries. Ordained men are called to a particular office by Christ (e.g., Rom. 10:15; Eph. 4:11), while nonordained men and all women in the church have a general office to serve the Lord in various capacities. If we did not have the chapter division between 1 Timothy 2:15 and 3:1 (which is a modern invention), this unique office context of Paul's statements on women in 2:11–12 would be more evident to us, since he proceeds directly to the requirements for male overseers of the church in 3:1–7.[23]

or to exercise authority over a man[24]

The Greek coordinating conjunction *oude* (and not, neither, cannot, either, even, neither, no, nor, nothing, or, then), plays more of an important role here than one might first imagine. Let us start with feminists, such as I. H. Marshall, who have argued that "authority" (Gr., *authentein*) has a negative connotation. In other words, they are claiming that Paul is not saying that women are not to teach because they would have authority over men in the Christian congregation, but that Paul is only against their negative authority in the church. Looking at the linguistic study first, we turn to H. S. Baldwin on the word *authentein*, "have or exercise authority," who demonstrated that the Greek word was very rare in the New Testament period. It occurs only once in the New Testament, in 1 Timothy 2:12. Outside of that, it only occurred a couple of times before 65 C.E.

We then look at the syntax by turning to A. J. Köstenberger on the word *oude*, "or," joining the words

---

[23] Clinton E. Arnold, Zondervan Illustrated Bible Backgrounds Commentary Volume 3: Romans to Philemon., 457-58 (Grand Rapids, MI. Zondervan, 2002).

[24] Second qualifier as to "in silence"

"teach" and "have authority." Köstenberger carried out thorough searches of the use of *oude* in the New Testament and Greek literature outside of the Greek New Testament, and he found over 100 parallels. His research showed that *oude* served as a coordinating conjunction, which linked verbs of like meaning. It was also discovered that either both were positive, or both were negative. An example can be found in Matthew 6:20 where Jesus said, "But lay up for yourselves treasures in heaven, where . . . thieves do not break in and (*oude*) steal." You immediately notice that "break in" and "steal" have a negative meaning. Therefore, if *didaskein* ("to teach") has a positive meaning, and *oude* is only known to link verbs of like meaning, we are only left with the conclusion both reasonably and syntactically *authentein* ("authority") must have a positive meaning as well. This, then, removes the argument by the feminist scholars, as Paul is not just prohibiting a negative exercise of authority by women over men in the Christian congregation, but rather the exercise of authority period. Simply put, men alone are to serve as elders and overseers in the congregation. 1 Timothy 3:2

"Man" (Gr., aner) is referring to "a man," not the more confined sense of the "husband." As in verse 8, "man" is being used as a distinction from a woman. That it is in the singular means that it is a reference to men in general, just as the singular γυνή *gune* ("woman") here and in verse 11 refers to women in general.

but to be in quietness

Thus far, it is all too clear that a woman may not teach on the Christian congregation, nor may she teach a man biblically, doctrinally. This is emphasized, "but to be in quietness." The *alla*, "but," is used here to mark a contrast to what came before, "not to teach or to exercise authority."

For those that would argue that we are only talking about specific types of authoritative teaching, this exhortation to 'be in silence,' would negate that argument. Of course, this does not rule out conversations before and after meetings, commenting at Bible studies, and singing. It is dealing explicitly with teaching and the exercise of authority.

2:12 Greek, Grammar & Syntax

> **2:12** Paul carries this injunction further by indicating that he does not permit women to teach and exercise authority over men. δέ is used here to indicate the contrast, "learn but not teach" (cf. 1 Cor. 14:34, where the desire to learn is not to be used to gain the privilege of speaking, and notice the close parallel of that passage, **οὐ γὰρ ἐπιτρέπεται αὐταῖς λαλεῖν**, to our passage). ἐπιτρέπω (NT 17x) means "allow, permit" someone (dative) to do something (infinitive; BAGD).
>
> Some have suggested that Paul conveys here only a note of personal disinclination (cf. Phillips's translation: "Personally, I don't allow"). But such a suggestion misunderstands the authoritativeness of ἐπιτρέπω when used by Paul (cf. Robertson: "Paul speaks authoritatively"), which is demonstrated by a close analysis of the three occurrences in Paul (1 Cor. 14:34, a parallel; 16:7, an action of the Lord; here). The strength of the prohibition here is underlined by Paul's appeal to the creation order (v. 13, γάρ); in 1 Cor. 14:34 the prohibition is correlated to "the law" (undoubtedly the same OT teaching as here in v. 13) and is further delineated by his covering statement in v. 37, "the things that I write to you are the Lord's commandment."

It has also been suggested that the present indicative form of ἐπιτρέπω indicates a temporal limitation and thus limits Paul's statement to the then and there of Ephesus. An examination of other occurrences of Paul's use of first person singular present indicative (Rom. 12:1, 3; 1 Cor. 4:16; 2 Cor. 5:20; Gal. 5:2, 3, Eph. 4:1; 1 Thes. 4:1; 5:14; 2 Thes. 3:6; 1 Tim. 2:1, 8) demonstrates that he uses it to give universal and authoritative instruction or exhortation (cf. especially Rom. 12:1; 1 Tim. 2:8).

As in vv. 9 and 11, so also here γυνή refers generally to any "woman," and this is probably highlighted by the use of anarthrous forms for both γυνή and ἀνήρ. Just as it was womanhood that required silence and submission in v. 11, so here also it is womanhood (vis-à-vis men) that is in view in the prohibition.

That which is not permitted is first of all διδάσκειν, "to teach," but not as an unqualified prohibition since the object "man" indicates a limitation, as does the immediate context, which has been dealing with religious instruction in the life of the church. To this can be compared Paul's commendation of women teaching other women (Tit. 2:3–5) and teaching their children and sons (2 Tim. 1:5; 3:14, 15; cf. Acts 16:1); he apparently also approved of the team effort of Priscilla and Aquila in explaining in private conversation ("they took him aside") to Apollos "the way of God more accurately" (Acts 18:25, 26). Just as v. 11 was not a demand for all learning to be done in silence, as an unqualified absolute, but was concerned with women's learning in the midst of the assembled people of God, so also the prohibition of teaching here has the same setting and perspective in view.

διδάσκειν (Pl.* 15x) means generally "to teach or instruct." Here the religious subject matter is assumed, and the persons (not) to be taught are "men," the implication being that women may not teach or exercise authority in or over the church (of which men are a part; cf. 1 Cor. 14:34, 35: "in the churches," "in church"). Other uses of the verb in 1 Timothy are in settings where Timothy is urged to teach as part of his ministry (4:11; 6:2), and others are also so urged in 2 Timothy (2:2), though in Titus (1:11) the activity may be somewhat more general. A similar authoritative note is found in Rom. 12:7; 1 Cor. 4:17; Gal. 1:12; [Eph. 4:21?]; Col. 1:28; 2:7; 2 Thes. 2:15. In Col. 3:16 Paul does not restrict teaching to ministers in distinction from other Christians, and in other places he uses the verb in the most general sense (but still with a certain note or overtone of authority indicated [1 Cor. 11:14] or implied [Rom. 2:21]). In 1 Cor. 14:34, 35, the instruction that women "keep silence" is given in the context of various Christians getting up and speaking. Both there and here Paul's prohibition of women teaching would prevent them from serving as elders or ministers, but it is unwarranted to limit it to such a restriction from office-bearing. Paul uses functional language ("to teach") rather than office language ("a bishop") to express the prohibition. Here he prohibits women from publicly teaching men, and thus teaching the church.

οὐδέ joins the second infinitive to the first under οὐκ ἐπιτρέπω, whose negative is now conveyed in οὐδέ itself. Robertson (*Grammar*, 1185) indicates that "in accord with the copulative use of δέ we frequently have οὐδέ and μηδέ in the continuative sense, carrying on the negative with no idea of contrast" (cf., e.g., Mt. 6:26). Therefore, οὐδέ here may be rendered "nor" *(KJV, NEB)* or for English stylistic reasons "or" *(NASB, RSV, TEV, NIV)*.

αὐθεντεῖν** (a biblical hapax; see Knight, "ΑΥΘΕΝΤΕΩ" and the response by Wilshire, "TLG Computer"), once thought to be unique to Christian literature (e.g., Thayer, *Lexicon*), occurs in the papyrus *BGU* 1208:38 (27 b.c.) and in Philodemus, *Rhetoric* 2 (first century b.c.; see BAGD for further documentation and later occurrences) and is referred to as Hellenistic (Ἑλληνικῶς) over against Attic αὐτοδικεῖν by the second-century a.d. Attic lexicographer Moeris (ed. J. Pierson [1759], 58; [43 in 1831 edition]; cf. also the account of the word and its meaning and that of related words, especially αὐθέντης, in MM; Deissmann, *Light*, 88f.; Robertson, IV, 570; MHT II, 278). Contrary to the suggestion of *KJV*'s "to usurp authority" and BAGD's alternative, "domineer" (so also *NEB*), the use of the word shows no inherent negative sense of grasping or usurping authority or of exercising it in a harsh or authoritative way, but simply means "to have or exercise authority" (BAGD; LSJM: "to have full power or authority over"; cf. Preisigke, *Wörterbuch* I, 235f., giving three nuances for four different papyri, all in the sphere of the above definition; cf. finally Lampe, *Lexicon*, whose four main meanings are in the same orbit; so *NASB, RSV, TEV, NIV:* "to have authority").

Paul refers, then, with αὐθεντεῖν to exercise of a leadership role or function in the church (the contextual setting), and thus by specific application the office of ἐπίσκοπος/πρεσβύτερος, since the names of these offices (especially ἐπίσκοπος) and the activities associated with them (cf., e.g., 3:4, 5; 5:17; Tit. 1:9ff.; Acts 20:17, 28ff.) indicate the exercise of authority. It is noteworthy, however, that Paul does not use "office" terminology here (bishop/presbyter) but functional terminology (teach/exercise authority). It is thus the activity that he prohibits, not just the office (cf. again 1 Cor. 14:34, 35).

ἀνήρ is used here, as in v. 8, to refer to "man" in distinction from woman, not in its more restricted sense of "husband." The singular refers to men in general, just as γυνή refers here and in v. 11 to women in general. The genitive case of ἀνδρός agrees with the nearer infinitive, which like other verbs of ruling and governing takes the genitive (BDF §177; Robertson, *Grammar*, 510), though the noun qualifies not only the second infinitive, αὐθεντεῖν, but also the first, διδάσκειν, in accordance with normal Greek usage (cf. Acts 8:21, where as here οὐδέ is used; see also Smyth, *Grammar* §1634, which gives an example of two infinitives joined by οὐδέ with a common object written only once).

That a woman may not teach in the church, or teach a man, is underlined by the addition of ἀλλ' εἶναι ἐν ἡσυχίᾳ. The adversative particle ἀλλά indicates that this clause is contrasted with what precedes (not to teach or exercise authority *but* to be in silence). Some have suggested that Paul is only ruling out teaching or exercise of authority apart from a man's oversight, or just a certain type of authoritative teaching. The insistence here on silence seems to rule out all these solutions. The clause as a whole describes the status of a woman not in relation to every aspect of the gathered assembly (i.e., praying, prophesying, singing, etc.; cf. again 1 Cor. 11:5) but specifically in respect to that with which it is contrasted, i.e., teaching (and the exercise of authority), just as the

> first occurrence of ἐν ἡσυχίᾳ applied to the learning/teaching situation (v. 11).[25]

1 Timothy 2:13 Updated American Standard Version (UASV)

[13] For Adam was formed first, then Eve,

13 For Adam was formed first, then Eve[26]

The conjunction "for" (Gr., γάρ, gar) signifies that we are about to get the first reason as to why for the command in the previous verse. We go again to Paul's words to the Corinthians because he offers the same reason for man's headship over women. "But I want you to understand that the head of every man is Christ, the head of a wife is her husband, and the head of Christ is God." (1 Cor. 11:3) Paul goes on to say, "For man was not made from woman, but woman from man. Neither was man created for woman, but woman for man." 1 Corinthians 11:8-9

The Hebrew and Greek word "Adam" is a transliteration and occurs as "man," "mankind," as well as the proper name of the first human male created by God. The use here is not a generic use like "mankind," but rather as the "male" was created "first" (Gr., πρῶτος, protos, predicate adjective), making the contrasting point that "Adam" or the "male" was created before the female and is the chronological priority over the female. In other words, Paul is making the point that because the male was created first, it carries with it the head, the leadership role. Not only

---

[25] George W. Knight, *The Pastoral Epistles: A Commentary on the Greek Text*, New International Greek Testament Commentary (Grand Rapids, MI; Carlisle, England: W.B. Eerdmans; Paternoster Press, 1992), 140–142.

[26] Causal connection: First reason as to why women are to learn in silence (submission [vs. 11] rather than "teach" or have "authority" [vs. 12] since the beginning)

did God create Adam, the male first, but also he created the female from Adam, for the sake of Adam, to serve as a helper or complement to Adam. (Gen. 2:18–25; 1 Cor. 11:8-9)

Embedded within Adam was the natural inclination to take the lead, while Eve's natural inclination was to follow that lead. Her body was created from a piece of Adam's body, his name in Hebrew is ish, meaning "man," while hers was derived from his name, ishah, meaning "woman" (literally, a female man). As Paul makes all too clear, we do not sidestep the order of things when it comes to our worship in the Christian congregation. We are given one time where Eve took the lead without consulting her head, resulting in her being deceived by the serpent (Satan, John 8:44; Rev. 12:9). Eve led the way into sin, and Adam followed. Since the feminist movement of the 1960s, the divorce rate has risen steeply. We have asked women to go against their natural inclination to follow or support the leadership of their head, resulting in fractured families and homes, as well as the partial reason for some of the fragmentation of the Christian congregation.

Head Covering Excursion

Many Christians understand this section as a cultural issue that had an application in first-century society but does not apply today. They see it in much the same way as 1 Corinthians 11, which also uses the Genesis account as a basis for women covering their heads in public worship.[27]

---

[27] Knute Larson, vol. 9, I & II Thessalonians, I & II Timothy, Titus, Philemon, Holman New Testament Commentary, 170-71 (Nashville, TN: Broadman & Holman Publishers, 2000).

This would be a mistaken notion. It is not culturally bound to the first-century C.E. Women are not to teach or exercise authority over a man. Women are to wear a head covering under certain circumstances. They are both permanent and are applicable today. As was stated earlier and will be stated again, God is outside of time and culture.

The wearing of a head covering has a spiritual import within the Christian congregation. Paul, whose written word is inspired of God, lays out the God designated principle of how headship was/is to take place in the Christian congregation, saying, "I want you to understand that the head of every man is Christ, the head of a wife is her husband, and the head of Christ is God." Paul informs the Corinthians, and by extension, us that the head covering is "a symbol of authority" that women are required to wear that man is their head when she "prays or prophesies." In other words, if a woman is called on to substitute for her husband or a man that relates to some form of worship, she should wear a head covering. – 1 Corinthians 11:4-6, 10.

For example, all families should have their own family Bible studies within their home. Suppose the husband is not present for any reason (deceased, separated, divorced, or called away), and the wife has to conduct the family study. In that case, she is not obligated to wear a head covering because the husband is not present. The same would hold for saying the family prayer at meals as well. If for some reason, the husband is present but is unable to speak (maybe throat issues), she would wear the head covering. The wife would not have to wear a head covering with the children, as the woman is divinely authorized to teach the children. – Proverbs 1:8; 6:20.

However, if the husband is not present, and one of the children is a son, an adult born-again Christian, he would conduct the study. If the son were a younger born-again

Christian, she would then wear a head covering. (1 Timothy 2:12) Since the son is a Christian, he is to receive his instruction from other male Christians.

Again, if a woman is needed to substitute for her husband or a man related to some form of worship, she should wear a head covering. Within the congregation, women may be called on to teach a Bible study group for women or children because there are not enough men, which means she would have to wear a head covering. If the woman is in a Bible study group that a male conducts, she does not have to wear a head covering to participate. Outside of the Christian congregation, both men and women are obligated to preach and teach the unbeliever, meaning she does not have to wear a head covering. – Matthew 24:14; 28:19, 20.

2:13 Greek, Grammar & Syntax

2:13 The ground for the prohibition is now given: It is the order of the creation of Adam and Eve as the archetypes of man and woman and the implication of this order for headship and submission in such relationships. (The conjunction γάρ signifies that the statement that follows provides the reason for the previous command; cf. BAGD s.v. 1.) The verse is a terse statement of an argument that Paul has used before in connection with the headship of man to woman in 1 Cor. 11:3ff.

Ἀδάμ is the transliteration of the Hebrew word used in Genesis as the name of the first man created by God (first in the Hebrew text at Gn. 1:26; first in the LXX at Gn. 2:16; cf. 1 Cor. 15:45: "the first man, Adam"). It is used in our passage not of generic "mankind," as in Gn. 1:26, 27, but of man = male, as distinct from Eve (cf. especially Gn. 2:20ff.). πρῶτος, used here as a predicate adjective (cf. BAGD s.v. 1a; Robertson, *Grammar*, 657; BDF §243), indicates both the absolute priority of Adam in God's creation and, most of all, in the contrast here of Adam to Eve (εἶτα Εὕα), his priority to her. πλάσσω** (Rom. 9:20; 1 Tim. 2:13; both seem to reflect the OT usage) means "form" or "mold" and is the verb used by the LXX in Gn. 2:7, 8, 15 (v. 15 without a Hebrew equivalent) of the creation of Adam. εἶτα (NT 13x) is used here, as is predominantly the case in the NT, as a temporal adverb meaning "then." It is found in the "first … then …" construction here and in 3:10 (BAGD s.v. 1). Εὕα** (2 Cor. 11:3; 1 Tim. 2:13) is the Greek transliteration (sometimes Εὕα) of Hebrew *ḥawwâh*, the name of the woman formed from Adam (first so named in Gn. 3:20, where the LXX renders it Ζωή: the first use of Εὕα in the LXX is in 4:1).

It is evident, then, that Paul has Genesis 2 in mind here, just as he has Genesis 3 in mind in the next verse, as is evidenced by his use of LXX terms (especially πλάσσω). The appeal to what God does (or says) with Adam and Eve in the creation account as an indication of God's will with reference to men and women in general is similar to the argument Jesus uses in demonstrating that God intends permanence for marriage between men and women (Mt. 19:4–6).

With this brief statement on the order of creation Paul appeals to the whole of the creation narrative, as is indicated by his fuller treatment in 1 Cor. 11:8–9 (cf. Dodd, *According to the Scriptures*). This whole account would include "a helper suitable for him [i.e., for man, Adam]"; (Gn. 2:18) and the significance of the naming of the woman: "She shall be called Woman, because she was taken out of Man" (2:23). Paul explicitly specifies that the woman was "taken out of" (ἐκ) the man and created to

> help, or to be "for" (διά), the man in his fuller statement in 1 Corinthians. So it is not mere chronology ("first ... then ...") that Paul appeals to here but what is entailed in this chronology. (That drawing such implications from chronological priority is not foreign to the OT is seen from the similar, but different, appeals to the rights of primogeniture [see I. H. Marshall, *NBD* 377f.; J. E. Rosscup, *ZPEB* II, 540f.; R. de Vaux, *Ancient Israel*, 41f.].)[28]

1 Timothy 2:14 Updated American Standard Version (UASV)

[14] and Adam was not deceived, but the woman was deceived and came to be in transgression.

The Bible makes it clear that Satan, by using the Serpent as his mouthpiece, did, in fact, deceive Eve. Satan's deception was to the point where Eve came to believe that by rebelling against God, she could become godlike in being able to determine for herself what was good and what was bad, that is, independence. (Genesis 3:4-5) Assuming this to be true, she sinned. Nevertheless, God held her responsible, and so she was sentenced to die. Why? Because even though Satan lied and deceived her, she was at all times fully aware of God's command. Eve was never forced to disobey.

On the contrary, she was a perfect human with her full faculties, remained in control of her actions, having the ability to resist Satan's influence at any time. In fact, Adam, the head of her, had informed her of the tree's prohibition

---

[28] George W. Knight, *The Pastoral Epistles: A Commentary on the Greek Text*, New International Greek Testament Commentary (Grand Rapids, MI; Carlisle, England: W.B. Eerdmans; Paternoster Press, 1992), 142–143.

to the point that Eve stressed the prohibition even further by saying, "God said, 'You shall not eat from it, nor shall you touch it, lest you die.'" (Genesis 3:3) Moreover, she had every opportunity to ask her husband, Adam, if what Satan was saying was, in fact, true.

We need to recall that this is a personal letter to a specific group of fellow believers and a very close companion, Timothy, who had been traveling and working with Paul for about fifteen years. Paul told Timothy of his mission for him, "I urged you when I was going to Macedonia, remain at Ephesus so that you may charge certain ones not to teach different doctrine." (1 Tim. 1:3) Timothy was to search out the truth from the deception, identifying these ungodly men, these false teachers, restoring order among the chaos. Part of this chaos was likely that the women in the Ephesian Christian congregation sought to usurp the spiritual leaders' authority because the false teachers were deceiving them. Once again, we have the female going beyond her role in life. Thus, we have the reference to Eve's deception.

Man was given the leadership role in the Garden of Eden. He was given the leadership role in the church and in the home. It was designed this way from the beginning. Women are expected to accept their role within creation silently, understanding that this truth removes troubles, brings unity, and eliminates uncertainties.

Genesis 3:6 Excursion

Almost all translations translate Genesis 3:6 as follows.

Genesis 3:6 English Standard Version (ESV)

⁶ So when the woman saw that the tree was good for food, and that it was a delight to the eyes, and that the tree was to be desired to make one wise, **she took of its fruit**

and ate, and she also gave some to her husband <u>who was with her</u>, and he ate.

Genesis 3:6 Lexham English Bible (LEB)

6 When the woman saw that the tree was good for food and that it was a delight to the eyes, and the tree was desirable to make one wise, then **she took from its fruit and she ate. And she gave it also to her husband <u>with her</u>**, and he ate.

Genesis 3:6 American Standard Version (ASV)

⁶ And when the woman saw that the tree was good for food, and that it was a delight to the eyes, and that the tree was to be desired to make one wise, **she took of the fruit thereof, and did eat; and she gave also unto her husband <u>with her</u>**, and he did eat.

Genesis 3:6 New American Standard Bible (NASB)

⁶ When the woman saw that the tree was good for food, and that it was a delight to the eyes, and that the tree was desirable to make one wise, **she took from its fruit and ate; and she gave also to her <u>husband</u> with her**, and he ate.

As you can see from these English translations, the plain sense of the text is, Adam was with her. This creates a real Bible difficulty. Before I delve into why, I will say that if almost all of the translations are in agreement, generally, this should be respected, and accepted. It is doubtful that the very best Hebrew and Greek scholars of the past 100 years are all mistaken. The difficulty arises because, if Eve and Adam are standing there before the tree of knowledge, as the serpent spoke to Eve, it means that Adam, the head, was very much involved in this process. Think as you read this commentary below, trying to rationalize how the situation played out, with the both of them being there.

> Eve "was indeed deceived," but Adam "was not deceived." Of course, this cannot be taken absolutely. It must mean something on this order: Adam was not deceived in the manner in which Eve was deceived. See Gen. 3:4–6. She listened directly to Satan; he did not. She sinned before he did. She was the leader. He was the follower. She led when she should have followed; that is, she led in the way of sin, when she should have followed in the path of righteousness.[29]

The reason for the difficulty is this; they are taking it as though Adam and Eve are standing before the tree of knowledge of good and evil, and the serpent, Satan, starts to speak to Eve. They carry on a conversation, with Adam simply passively listening. Satan deceives Eve, but Adam is not deceived, yet he does not argue with the serpent, snatch the fruit from Eve, but instead just stands there letting Eve each fruit, knowing she will die. Really? I just cannot see how that can rationally be the case. I would argue that Eve was alone before Adam joined her.

Was Adam standing beside Eve when she had the conversation with the serpent when she was deceived and chose to rebel against God? The Bible shows no indication that this is the case. The translations above make it appear that way, though, "she took of its fruit and ate, and she also <u>gave</u> some to her husband who was with her, and he ate."

The Hebrew verb translated as "gave" is in the imperfect waw consecutive. As a result, it points to a temporal or logical sequence (usually called an "imperfect sequential"). Hence, a Bible translator or committee can

---

[29] William Hendriksen and Simon J. Kistemaker, vol. 4, Exposition of the Pastoral Epistles, New Testament Commentary, 110 (Grand Rapids: Baker Book House, 1953-2001).

translate the several occurrences of the waw, which tie together the chain of events in verse 6, with "and" as well as other transitional words, such as "subsequently," "then," "after that," afterward," and "so."

Genesis 3:6 English Standard Version (ESV)

6 So when the woman saw that the tree was good for food, **and** that it was a delight to the eyes, **and** that the tree was to be desired to make one wise, she took of its fruit and ate, **and** she also gave some to her husband who was with her, **and** he ate.

Genesis 3:6 Updated American Standard Version (ESV)

6 So when the woman saw that the tree was good for food, **and** that it was a delight to the eyes, **and** that the tree was to be desirable to make one wise, **and** she took of its fruit and ate, **then** she also gave some to her husband when with her, **and** he ate.

One has to ask themselves. Would Adam have passively stood beside his wife Eve, listening to the conversation between her and the serpent, as the serpent spewed forth lies and malicious talk of Satan through this serpent, especially when Paul tells us explicitly that the serpent did not deceive Adam? Adam just stood there and remained silent? Adam just chose not to interrupt the peddling of lies. Listen to the Bible scholar below; he sure thinks this is reasonable.

> Genesis 3:6 makes it clear that he was "with her" during the interchange with the serpent, but he remained silent. He should have interrupted. He should have chased the serpent off. And when it comes down to it, when he is offered the fruit himself, he eats it—no questions asked, no protests given. Adam and Eve together rebelled

against their Creator, so they both suffer the horrible consequences.[30]

The conversation with the serpent reveals that Adam had previously carried out his responsibilities as the head, informing her of the command not to eat from the tree. (Gen. 3:3) It seems far more likely that Satan, through the serpent, ignored this headship, going after the newer person in the Garden of Eden, Eve, when she was alone. Eve later replied, "The serpent deceived me, and I ate."

Let us accept that I am mistaken, and it should be translated, "and she also gave some to her husband who was with her."

Adam need not be clear on the other side of the Garden; he could have just been out of hearing range and still have been with her. Suppose he was across the field, visually in sight but out of hearing range, it could still be said that he was with her. Husbands, have you ever been in a huge store with your wife, like Wal-Mart, and at the same time you are on one side of the store (lawn-garden or automotive), and she is on the other side of the store. If you were to say you were with your wife at Wal-Mart, would that mean that you were necessarily standing right beside her? Say an issue came up in the store, so you walked over. The Garden of Eden was no small place, like a city park, but more like the size of a state park, possibly 18,000 acres of land and 3,000 acres of water. If Adam were in eyesight but out of hearing range, it could still be said that he was with her. She could have called him over after her transgression, at which point, he demonstrated that his love for her was greater than that of his Creator, and so he ate.

---

[30] Longman III, Tremper (2005-05-12). How to Read Genesis (How to Read Series How to Read) (p. 111). Intervarsity Press – A. Kindle Edition.

14 and Adam was not deceived

Adam was absolutely not deceived; he simply chose that his love was greater for Eve than it was for his Creator. Paul is not shifting the blame on Eve; it is Adam, who was responsible for sin old age and death entering the world of humankind. (Rom 5:12, 19; 1 Cor. 15:22) Unlike Eve, he was not deceived by the lie that they would not die or that God was withholding good from them, such as special knowledge. Both Adam and Eve intentionally and willfully went in the course of self-resolve, rebellion against God. Adam's sin was far more grievous than Eve's. Moreover, it is his status as the head of Eve and the human race, which laid the full accountability at his feet.

but the woman was deceived

Genesis 3:13 has Eve herself stating, "The serpent deceived me, and I ate." Eve had been completely deceived by the serpent, consumed by the desire of the eyes, mind, and heart for the prospects lay before her, having only to eat of the tree, and she transgressed the law of God. This tree of knowledge of good and evil looked no different from any other tree; it was a mere symbol of God's sovereignty. However, look again at Eve's words, after she succumbed to the serpent's deception, "So when the woman saw that the tree was good for food, and that it was a delight to the eyes, and that the tree was to be desired to make one wise."

Both Adam and Eve had a natural desire to do good. We, in this imperfect age and flesh, have the natural desire to do bad. Listen to the words of one of the greatest Christians ever to walk this earth. "So I find it to be a law that when I want to do right, evil lies close at hand. For I delight in the law of God, in my inner being, but I see in my members another law waging war against the law of my mind and making me captive to the law of sin that dwells in my members. Wretched man that I am! Who will deliver me from this body of death?" (Rom. 7:21-24) However, Paul knew the real source of his strength in weakness, as he goes on to answer his question, "Thanks be to God through Jesus Christ our Lord! So then, I myself serve the law of God with my mind, but with my flesh, I serve the law of sin."

With Eve's natural desire to be toward good, it means that she really had to go against the grain to violate her conscience. James gives us an answer about how that can happen, even to a perfect person, with the natural desire toward good. "Each person is tempted when he is lured and enticed by his own desire. Then desire when it has conceived gives birth to sin, and sin when it is fully grown brings forth death." (Jam 1:14-15) The human eye is a wonder of creation. Still, it is also a direct channel of communication to the mind, which affects the emotions and actions, the figurative heart, and the seat of motivation. Satan tempted Eve by having her look at a tree that was no different, giving it a whole other look with the desire of the eyes. He did the same thing with Jesus, trying to persuade him to sin by reaching out inappropriately for things Jesus saw with his eyes. (Lu 4:5-7) The apostle John warns us,

1 John 2:16-17 Updated American Standard Version (UASV)

[16] For all that is in the world, the lust of the flesh and the lust of the eyes and the boastful pride of life, is not from the Father, but is from the world. [17] The world is passing away, and its lusts; but the one who does the will of God remains forever.

and came to be in transgression

Sin can be in the form of a "transgression." The Greek *parabasis* basically means "overstepping." It is an "act of deviating from an established boundary or norm,"[31] especially concerning law.

2:14 Greek, Grammar & Syntax

2:14 καί joins this verse to the preceding. Paul now appeals to the fall as an event that demonstrates in the most absolute way the dire consequences of a reversal of leadership roles. Just as v. 13 reflects the events and terminology of Genesis 2, so v. 14 reflects Genesis 3 and the terms used there (especially ἀπατάω).

ἀπατάω** (Eph. 5:6; here; Jas. 1:26) means "deceive" or "mislead" and occurs in the LXX of Genesis only at 3:13 in the woman's statement: "The serpent deceived me." καὶ Ἀδὰμ οὐκ ἠπατήθη is not meant to deny Adam's sin or participation in the fall (cf. Rom. 5:12ff.; 1 Cor. 15:21, 22) but to indicate, as the Genesis narrative does, that he sinned willfully, not as a result of deception (Gn. 3:6, 12). To this Paul contrasts (δέ= "but") the woman's deception. ἡ γυνή is probably used instead of "Eve" because it is used in the LXX of the Genesis 3 account (vv. 1, 2, 4, 6, 12, 13, 15, 16, 17; "Eve" appears in v. 20, only after the temptation / fall / judgment account) and also perhaps to begin to make the transition from Eve as a type to women in general (to whom this section is addressed). (γυνή is used in the statement about the seed of the woman in Gn. 3:15 [cf. both Hebrew and LXX].) The argument would then proceed in three steps: from "Eve" to "the woman" (singular as a transition from "Eve" to "women") to

---

[31] William Arndt, Frederick W. Danker and Walter Bauer, A Greek-English Lexicon of the New Testament and Other Early Christian Literature, 3rd ed., 758 (Chicago: University of Chicago Press, 2000).

plural "women" in v. 15 (cf. Ridderbos). The compound form ἐξαπατάω, which similarly means "deceive" or "lead astray," may be used with regard to "the woman" in contrast with the preceding uncompounded form (with "Adam") for emphasis; but it also may simply be a stylistic change reflecting Paul's preference, since he uses the same compound verb in reference to Eve in 2 Cor. 11:3 as well. The basis for Paul's affirmation is the woman's statement in Gn. 3:13: "The serpent deceived me, and I ate."

The last part of the verse indicates the state of affairs resulting from the deception: the woman "fell into transgression" (*NASB*; cf. BAGD s.v. ἐν 14d) or "became a transgressor" (*RSV;* BAGD s.v. παράβασις [612]). παράβασις is used of the overstepping of set limits and therefore more tersely "transgression," in the NT always transgression against God's law or standard. Eve, by being deceived, took and ate the prohibited fruit and thus came into transgression. γέγονεν (perfect tense) indicates, with the prepositional phrase, the new condition into which she entered.

V. 14 thus shows by a negative example the importance of heeding the respective roles established by God in the creation of Eve from Adam. This adds to v. 13 (with καί) an example rather than a separate basis for Paul's argument. Thus, Paul argues not from creation and fall but from creation, and then illustrates this argument, albeit negatively, from the fall (cf. God's judgment on

> Adam: "Because you have listened to the voice of your wife," Gn. 3:17).[32]

1 Timothy 2:15 Updated American Standard Version (UASV)

15 Yet she will be saved through childbearing, if they continue in faith and love and holiness, with soundness of mind.[33]

15 Yet she will be saved through childbearing

No one would reasonably believe women are saved by simply bearing children. This being "saved" is not meant as eternal salvation, but more of being kept safe. You may remember the woman, "who had suffered from a discharge of blood for twelve years came up behind him and touched the fringe of his garment," and was healed. Well, it literally says, "your faith has saved you." However, translations render it as "your faith has made you well." Jesus was not telling this woman that her faith gave her eternal salvation but that she had been healed and made safe from this ongoing affliction by her faith. The same is true of what Paul is saying here, for women in the Christian congregation. Women have a role to play in the marriage arrangement, which is to bear children and raise them with the teachings of God. If you encompass that with the preaching and teaching work of the Great Commission and congregation responsibilities, she will not have time to feed off the spirit

---

[32] George W. Knight, *The Pastoral Epistles: A Commentary on the Greek Text*, New International Greek Testament Commentary (Grand Rapids, MI; Carlisle, England: W.B. Eerdmans; Paternoster Press, 1992), 143–144.

[33] σώφρων, ον, gen. ονος strictly having a sound or healthy mind; as having ability to curb desires and impulses so as to produce a measured and orderly life self-controlled, sensible.—Timothy Friberg, Barbara Friberg and Neva F. Miller, vol. 4, Analytical Lexicon of the Greek New Testament, Baker's Greek New Testament Library, 373 (Grand Rapids, MI: Baker Books, 2000).

of this world that encourages women to forgo a family for a career, nor will she have time to desire the position of pastoring a congregation. Moreover, her role in the family will keep her safe from being an idle gossiper and interfere in other people's affairs. (1 Timothy 5:11-15) The context of 1 Timothy is 2:15 is verse 9 says that "women should adorn themselves in respectable apparel, with modesty and self-control, not with braided hair and gold or pearls or costly attire." Paul's additional counsel, in chapter five, has this to say about the unmarried women, that they are "idlers, going about from house to house, and not only idlers but also gossips and busybodies, saying what they should not."

if they continue in faith and love and holiness, with soundness of mind.

Turning again to the fifth chapter of this first letter to Timothy, Paul goes over some of the stumbling blocks that women (unmarried) suffer from, "idlers, going about from house to house, and not only idlers but also gossips and busybodies, saying what they should not." He then gives them the following advice, "I would have younger widows marry, bear children, manage their households, and give the adversary no occasion for slander." Many young women stumble out of the faith, "straying after Satan," because they are idle from their responsibilities that they were given by God.

To be "sound in mind" comprises displaying good sense, being able to judge between right and wrong, modest, sensible in our speech and actions. It also means that women and men are to let God's Word be the guide to our thinking and actions. Roman 12:2

In conclusion, the natural reading of 1 Timothy 2:12 is that Paul in his apostolic authority prohibits women from teaching and exercising authority over a man, which means that women cannot serve as pastors or elders in the Christian congregation. We are not to mold to the pressures of the modern-day feminist movement because this position goes back to before the fall, has always been applicable, and will always be applicable.

Men serve as overseers, servants (deacons). In the discussion of "gifts in men" given by Christ to the congregation, there is no mention of women. The words "apostles," "prophets," "evangelizers," "shepherds," and "teachers" are all in the masculine gender. (Eph 4:8, 11) Ephesians 4:11 is rendered by the American Translation: "And he has given us some men as apostles, some as prophets, some as missionaries, some as pastors and teachers."—Compare Moffets; also see Ps 68:18, ESV, UASV, NASB, and ASV.

In complete harmony with this, when the apostle Paul wrote to Timothy about who would qualify for the positions of "overseers" (*episkopoi*), who were also "older men" (presbyteroi), and of "servants" (*diakonoi*) in the Christian congregation, he clearly states that they must be men and, if married, 'the husband of one wife.' No treatment by any of the apostles discusses any office of "deaconess" (diakonissa).—1 Tim. 3:1-13; Tit. 1:5-9; compare Ac 20:17, 28; Phil. 1:1.

While it is true that Phoebe is mentioned (Rom. 16:1) as a "minister" (*diakonos*, without the Greek definite article), it is obvious that she was not an elected female servant in the Christian congregation, because the Scriptures make no stipulation for such. The apostle did not tell the Christian congregation to take instructions from her but, rather, to accept her favorably and to "help her in whatever task she may have need from you, for she herself also has been a helper of many, even me myself." (Rom. 16:2, UASV; See also LEB, NASV, ASV) When Paul referred to her as a minister, it clearly had something to do with her sharing the Gospel, and he was speaking of Phoebe as a female minister who was connected to the Christian congregation in Cenchreae. (Compare Ac 2:17-18) Some translators mistakenly view the term in an official function and therefore render it "deaconess" (Rom. 16:1-2; RS, JB, footnote: ESV, LEB, NASB, CSB). However, the Scriptures do not make any provision for female servants. Goodspeed's translation sees the term in a general function and translates it "helper." However, as was stated above, Paul's reference is apparently to something having to do with the spreading of the Gospel, the Christian ministry.

What About Romans 16:7?

Romans 16:7 Updated American Standard Version (UASV)
⁷ Greet Andronicus and Junias, my kinsmen and my fellow prisoners, who are well known among the apostles, who also were in Christ before me.

(Ju'ni·as)

Junias received a special greeting from Paul at the end of his letter to the Romans. (16:7) Andronicus and Junias were his "kinsmen." The Greek word used here (συγγενής) can mean "a man from one's own country," or "fellow countryman." The primary meaning is blood relative, including the extended family," of the same generation. The two were Paul's "fellow prisoners," meaning that they had been in prison with him somewhere. Paul calls them both "well known among the apostles," perhaps remembering their fine reputation with the apostles. Note that it does not call Andronicus and Junias apostles but only says that they were well known **among** the apostles. The Greek term (*episēmos*) rendered **well know** is a plural **masculine** adjective. Therefore, it could rightly be rendered, "men who are well known among the apostles."[34]

What About the Argument That Paul Wrote Those Things Because He Lived in a Patriarchal Society or Culture that Influenced Him?

No, it does not follow. First, what if the Bible was written today, we could make the same counterargument, saying Paul wrote this or that because of the liberal-progressive culture. Second, Paul himself clearly states that "All Scripture is inspired by God" (2 Tim. 3:16), and that "men spoke from God as they were carried along by the Holy Spirit." (2 Pet. 1:21) Yes, God allowed the authors to use their writing style, but what they wrote were God's thoughts, and clearly, God is not influenced by any human society or culture.

Was Deborah a Ruler of Ancient Israel?

In the Old Testament, Deborah was a prophetess[35] in Israel. Deborah, the wife of Lappidoth, **encouraged** Judge Barak in the work God assigned him. So, Deborah encourages judge Barak like a wife would **encourage** her pastor husband of the church, offering moral support. Deborah had yet one other responsibility as well. She was

---

[34] James Swanson, Dictionary of Biblical Languages with Semantic Domains: Greek (New Testament) (Oak Harbor: Logos Research Systems, Inc., 1997).

[35] Other prophetesses included Miriam, Huldah, and the wife of Isaiah. – Exodus 15:20; 2 Kings 22:14; Isaiah 8:3.

also apparently settling conflicts by giving God's answer to problems that had come up. – Judges 4:4-5.

Again, Deborah was a prophetess in Israel. There was never a female ruler or judge in ancient Israel. Deborah was a proclaimer of God's Word. Her being an Old Testament prophetess is not the same being a New Testament pastor (elder). She never taught the Word of God. The prophets were not the teachers who taught the Israelite people. They were given the responsibility of sharing God's Word. They were a spokesperson for God. It was the priests' and Levites' responsibility to teach God's law to the nation of Israel. (Lev. 10:11; 14:57; 2Ch 15:3; 35:3) Yes, Judges 4:4 tells us that "Now Deborah, **a prophetess**, the wife of Lappidoth, was **judging Israel** at that time." In the Old Testament, there was no hesitation in Israel to involve women as prophets. Women identified as prophets in ancient Israel were Miriam (Ex. 15:20), Deborah (Judg. 4:4), Huldah (2 Kings 22:14), Noadiah (Neh. 6:14), and the unnamed wife of Isaiah (Isa. 8:3). We could rightly add Hannah as well (1 Sam. 2:1–10). See also Anna in Luke 2:36. Lastly, Deborah was used to offer moral support for Barak, who was shirking his responsibilities.

What About the Women Who Claim That They Are Called to Pastor a Church? The Women Say, 'It Is Our Calling? Who Are You to Reject a Person Called by God?'

1 Corinthians 7:12 Updated American Standard Version (UASV)

¹² But to the rest **I say, not the Lord**, that if any brother has a wife who is an unbeliever, and she consents to live with him, he must not divorce her.

Notice that Paul is saying, I am inspired by God, so I can say this and the Lord (Jesus), did not touch on this, but I am. Let us take a look at the context and historical setting.

1 Timothy 2:12 Updated American Standard Version (UASV)
¹² But I do not permit a woman to teach or to exercise authority over a man, but to be in silence.

Here again, we notice in 1 Timothy 2:12 that Paul is exercising the authority that he has been given and his word is, in essence, God's Word. So, the Bible says so that you cannot pastor a church at any level, including deacons. The other thing to consider is what if a homosexual man says he has the gift to pastor a church, or a man with many wives says he has the gift to pastor a church. The Bible says homosexuality is a gross (very serious), unseemly, shameful sin and that the homosexual "will not inherit the kingdom of God." (Rom. 1:26-28; 1 Cor. 6:9) Not every emotion that moves one to think they are gifted to do something gets to carry that out. Just because you feel like you have the gift to do something, that goes not give you the right to overrule, set aside the Word of God. God said 'the office of the elder must be the husband of one wife ' (1 Tim. 3;2), which means the office is held out to men alone. The Bible is very clear that women are not to teach or exercise authority over men. There is absolutely no justification or any feeling of a calling for a woman to hold the office of pastor/teacher or to exercise that authority. No one's feelings of being called can conflict with the plain language of the Bible. If one is wrong, it will be the one who has the feeling of being called and all who participate in that sin.

As has been stated already women can be ministers or teachers in other capacities. They can evangelize and teach unbelievers, unbaptized boys, and girls regardless of baptism, and women in church Bible studies. They can serve as missionaries.

1 Corinthians 14::34 Updated American Standard Version (UASV)

[34] let the women keep silent in the congregations, for it is not permitted for them to speak, but let them be in subjection, as the Law also says.

What Did the Apostle Paul Mean Women to Keep Silent in the Congregations? Are the Women Not to Speak at All?

"Let the women keep silent in the congregations," wrote the apostle Paul. (1 Corinthians 14:34) What did Paul mean? He was not saying that they could not even speak at all, or that they could not teach in any capacity, which would require speaking? No. In fact, he that "they are to teach what is good" in certain capacities. (2 Timothy 1:5; Titus 2:3-5) Here in the letter to the Corinthians, Paul told not only women but also persons who had the gift of tongues and prophecy to "keep silent" when there was another believer who was speaking. (1 Corinthians 14:26-30, 33) It is possible that some of the Christian women may have been so thrilled because of the newfound faith that they spoke up with questions interrupting the brother who was speaking, which actually was the custom in the first century throughout the Roman Empire. But Paul was moved by the Holy Spirit to avoid disorder, Paul urged them "If there is anything they desire to learn, let them ask their husbands at home. For it is shameful for a woman to speak in church."—1 Corinthians 14:35.

CHAPTER 2 Was the Apostle Paul Against Women?

THE apostle "Paul's teachings have been used as the basis for much of the anti-female bias within the Christian … church." So said Judge Cecilie Rushton of Auckland, New Zealand, in a paper presented early in 1993 to the Commonwealth Law Conference at Cyprus. "His Epistle to Timothy," she added, "reveals his thinking: 'But I suffer not a woman to teach, nor to usurp authority over the man, but to be in silence.'" – 1 Timothy 2:12, *King James Version*.

The secular world, which includes the modern-day Christian feminists and feminist theologians, and liberal to moderate Christian scholarship, who view Paul and his writings as his human opinion of the role or station of women, as opposed to his being inspired and moved along by the Holy Spirit. When we consider all fourteen of Paul's Bible books, from the epistle to the Romans to the book of Hebrews, can it be said that the apostle Paul evidenced any anti-female bias? What was the context of the words of Paul to Timothy, "But I do not permit a woman to teach or to exercise authority over a man, but to be in silence." – 1 Timothy 2:12.

Context of 1 Timothy 2:12-13

One of the most important ways to find answers to our Bible questions is also one of the most neglected: Investigating the Bible account that may have given rise to the question. Examine it thoroughly, ensuring that we do not neglect to read the context, the surrounding material. Paul in the chapter after our chapter under consideration in First Timothy states, "but in case I am delayed, **I am**

writing so that you will know how one ought **to conduct himself in the household of God**, which is the church of the living God, **the pillar** and support **of the truth.**" (1 Tim. 3:15) Thus, Paul tells us that this section of his letter to Timothy is to serve as a guide as to how we are to conduct ourselves at church, it is in the context of the church. Below is an outline of the entire letter to Timothy. We can see our topic for discussion, our context, 1 Timothy 2:9-15 within the entirety of the letter.

SECTION OUTLINE ONE (1 TIMOTHY 1)

Paul opens his first letter to Timothy with a warning against false teaching and a set of instructions for Timothy.

I. The Well-Beloved of Paul (1:1–2): Timothy is Paul's beloved spiritual son in the faith.

II. The Warning by Paul (1:3–11): The apostle urges Timothy to remain in Ephesus so that he might counteract some false teachings in regard to the law of Moses.

A. **The perverting of the law of Moses** (3:1–7)

1. *The perverters* (1:3a): They are self-appointed "experts" of the law, going about spreading their poison.

2. *The perversion* (1:3b–7): These men have added a grievous mixture of myths, fables, and endless genealogies to the law.

B. **The purpose of the law of Moses** (3:8–11)

1. *It was not made to control saved people* (1:8a).

2. *It was made to control unsaved people* (1:8b–11).

III. The Witness by Paul (1:12–17): Here the apostle expresses his profound thanksgiving for God's faithfulness.

A. **What God did** (1:12, 14–15)

1. *He saved Paul (1:14–15).*

---

2. *He selected Paul (1:12).*

B. **When God did it** (1:13): At the time, the apostle was a blasphemer and violent persecutor of Christians.

C. **Why God did it (1:16–17): He did it to demonstrate his amazing grace to even the worst of sinners.**

IV. The Wisdom by Paul (1:18–20)

A. **What Timothy is to do (1:18–19b)**

1. *Fight the good fight (1:18).*

2. *Keep the faith (1:19a).*

3. *Maintain a clear conscience (1:19b).*

B. **What Hymenaeus and Alexander have done** (1:19c–20)

1. *Their perversion* (1:19c): They have made a shipwreck of their faith, bringing shame to the name of Christ.

2. *Their punishment* (1:20): Paul has delivered them over to Satan.

SECTION OUTLINE TWO (1 TIMOTHY 2)

Paul writes about proper worship of God.

I. The Worship of God (2:1–2, 8): Paul discusses the subject of prayer.

A. **For whom we should pray** (2:1–2a)

1. *For those in authority (2:2a)*

2. *For everyone (2:1)*

B. **Why we should pray (2:2b): "So that we can live in peace and quietness."**

C. **How we should pray** (2:8): "With holy hands lifted up to God, free from anger and controversy."

II. The Will of God (2:3–7)

A. **The mission** (2:3–4): "God … wants everyone to be saved."

B. **The mediator** (2:5): Jesus Christ stands between God and people.

C. **The method** (2:6): Salvation was effected by the death of Christ.

D. **The messenger** (2:7): Paul has been chosen by God to serve as a missionary to the Gentiles.

III. The Woman of God (2:9–15)

A. **Her responsibilities** (2:9–11)

1. *In matters of apparel* (2:9–10): She should dress modestly as one who professes to worship God.

2. *In matters of attitude* (2:11): She should listen and learn quietly and humbly.

B. **Her restrictions (2:12–14)**

1. *The rule* (2:12): The woman is not permitted to teach or have authority over a man.

2. *The reason* (2:13–14): Two factors are given.

a. The factor of the original creation (2:13): Adam was created before Eve.

b. The factor of the original corruption (2:14): Adam was not deceived by Satan as was the woman.

C. **Her redemption (2:15): She will be "saved" through childbearing and by living in faith, love, holiness, and modesty.**

SECTION OUTLINE THREE (1 TIMOTHY 3)

Paul gives qualifications for pastors and deacons in the church and gives a sixfold summary of Jesus' earthly ministry.

I. The Shepherds for the Church (3:1–13)

A. **Qualifications for a pastor** (3:1–7)

1. *Positive qualifications* (3:1–2, 3c–5, 7)

a. **He** must be above reproach (3:1–2a).

b. **He** must have only one wife and be faithful to her (3:2b).

c. **He** must be temperate, self-controlled, respectable, hospitable, and able to teach (3:2c).

d. **He** must be gentle and have a well-behaved family (3:3c–5).

e. **He** must be respected by those outside the church (3:7).

2. *Negative qualifications* (3:3a–3b, 3d, 6)

a. **He** must not be a heavy drinker (3:3a).

b. **He** must not be violent (3:3b).

c. **He** must not be proud (3:6b).

d. **He** must not be greedy (3:3d).

e. **He** must not be a new Christian (3:6a).

B. **Qualifications for a deacon (3:8–13)**

1. *Positive qualifications* (3:8a, 9–13)

a. **He** must be sincere and worthy of respect (3:8a).

b. **He** must be a man of spiritual depth (3:9).

c. **He** must be a man of proven character and ability (3:10).

d. **He** must be faithful to his wife, and his wife must be a woman of good character (3:11–13).

2. *Negative qualifications* (3:8b–8c)

a. **He** must not be a heavy drinker (3:8b).

b. **He** must not be greedy (3:8c).

II. The Sheep in the Church (3:14–15): Paul tells Timothy to instruct the congregation concerning how they should behave themselves in the house of God.

III. The Savior of the Church (3:16): In this single and supreme verse, Paul gives a sixfold summary of Jesus' earthly ministry.

A. He appeared in a body (3:16a).

B. He was vindicated by the Spirit (3:16b).

C. He was seen by angels (3:16c).

D. He was announced to the nations (3:16d).

E. He was believed on in the world (3:16e).

F. He was taken up into heaven (3:16f).

SECTION OUTLINE FOUR (1 TIMOTHY 4)

Paul contrasts two kinds of shepherds.

I. Godless Shepherds (4:1–5): Paul warns Timothy against false teachers.

A. Who they are (4:2): Hypocritical and lying religious leaders.

B. **What they will do** (4:1b–1c, 3)

1. *Abandon the faith* (4:1b)

2. *Follow teachings that come from lying spirits and demons* (4:1c)

3. *Forbid marriage and the eating of certain foods* (4:3)

C. When they will do it (4:1a): In the "last times" before Jesus' coming.

D. **Why they are wrong** (4:4–5)

1. *Everything God created is good and thus should not be rejected* (4:4).

2. *Everything God created is made holy by God's Word and by prayer* (4:5).

II. Godly Shepherds (4:6–16): Paul lists some dos and don'ts concerning Christian ministry.

A. **The don'ts** (4:7a, 12a, 14)

1. *Don't waste time arguing over foolish ideas and silly myths* (4:7a).

2. *Don't be intimidated because of your youth* (4:12a).

3. *Don't neglect your spiritual gift* (4:14).

B. **The dos (4:6, 7b–11, 12b–13, 15–16)**

1. *Warn the church members concerning apostasy* (4:6).

2. *Keep spiritually fit* (4:7b–11).

3. *Be a godly role model in all you do* (4:12b).

4. *Continue to publicly read, teach, and preach the Word of God (4:13).*

5. *Give yourself wholly to the ministry* (4:15).

6. *Keep close check on your own life* (4:16).

SECTION OUTLINE FIVE (1 TIMOTHY 5)

Paul gives advice concerning older and younger men, older and younger women, widows, and church elders.

I. The People (5:1–16): Paul gives advice concerning church members.

A. **In regard to older men** (5:1a): Treat them as respected fathers.

B. **In regard to younger men** (5:1b): Treat them as brothers.

C. **In regard to older women** (5:2a): Treat them as mothers.

D. **In regard to younger women** (5:2b): Treat them as sisters.

E. **In regard to widows** (5:3–16)

1. *Older widows* (5:3–10, 16)

a. Widows who are over sixty, godly, and have no living children (5:3, 5, 9–10, 16): These are to be honored and provided for.

b. Widows who have living children and grandchildren (5:4, 8, 16): They are to be cared for by their families.

c. Widows who are carnal and live only for pleasure (5:6–7): They are to receive no help.

2. *Younger widows* (5:11–15)

a. The rule (5:11–12, 14): Let them remarry and raise children.

b. The reason (5:13, 15): This will keep them from immorality and idle talk.

II. The Preachers (5:17–25): Paul's advice concerning church elders.

A. **Elders in general (5:17–22, 24–25)**

1. *They are worthy of double honor* (5:17–18).

2. *They must never be unjustly accused* (5:19–20, 24–25).

3. *They must be impartial* (5:21).

4. *They must be proven before being ordained* (5:22a).

5. *They must keep themselves pure* (5:22b).

B. **Timothy in particular** (5:23): "Drink a little wine for the sake of your stomach because you are sick so often."

SECTION OUTLINE SIX (1 TIMOTHY 6)

Paul addresses the workers, the wicked, the wise, and the wealthy. He closes his letter with some final instructions for Timothy.

I. Paul's Words to the People (6:1–10): Paul addresses four types of individuals.

A. **The workers** (6:1–2): Paul urges Christian servants to render faithful service to their masters, lest the name of God be slandered.

B. **The wicked** (6:3–5)

1. *They deny the faith* (6:3–4a).

2. *They are conceited and argumentative (6:4b).*

3. *They cause confusion, envy, and friction (6:4c).*

4. *They use spiritual things for financial gain (6:5).*

C. **The wise** (6:6–8): They realize that godliness with contentment is great gain.

D. **The wealthy** (6:9–10)

1. *The desire* (6:10): "The love of money is at the root of all kinds of evil."

> 2. *The destruction* (6:9): This kind of greed, if unchecked, will result in ruin and destruction.
>
> II. Paul's Words to the Pastor (6:11–21)
>
> A. **What Timothy is to do** (6:11–14, 17–21)
>
> 1. *Flee from evil, and follow after good* (6:11).
>
> 2. *Fight the good fight of faith* (6:12).
>
> 3. *Faithfully fulfill your ministry* (6:13–14, 20a).
>
> 4. *Warn the rich* (6:17–19).
>
> a. What they should do (6:17–18)
>
> (1) Don't trust in your money (6:17).
>
> (2) Use it to help others (6:18).
>
> b. Why they should do it (6:19): God will reward them both on earth and in heaven.
>
> 5. *Reject godless philosophies* (6:20b–21).
>
> B. **For whom Timothy is to do it** (6:15–16): **God.**
>
> 1. *The blessed and only Almighty God* (6:15a)
>
> 2. *The King of Kings* (6:15b)
>
> 3. *The Lord of Lords* (6:15c)
>
> 4. *The immortal and invisible God* (6:16a)
>
> 6. *The One dwelling in unapproachable light* (6:16b)[36]

If you have not done so, please go back and consider our verses under consideration, 2:9-15, considering what comes before and after, as well as the flow of the letter so that we can grasp our section in its context.

---

[36] H. L. Willmington, *The Outline Bible* (Wheaton, IL: Tyndale House Publishers, 1999), 1 Ti 1–6:16.

Paul the Apostle

Out of our 27 books of the Greek New Testament, 14 of them were authored by the apostle Paul. Another factor that evidences the Holy Spirit on him was the fact that he could speak in many tongues. In addition, he had supernatural visions. (1 Cor. 14:18; 2 Cor. 12:1-5) Paul's unselfish, self-denying, whole-souled, and loving example created a close bond of warm brotherly love and affection between him and the Christians of his day. (Acts 20:37-38) Thus, his writings were the product of the Holy Spirit, which would include what he had to say about the women within the Christian congregation, "all Scripture ... inspired by God and profitable for teaching." (2 Tim. 3:16) Yes, this is what God had to say about Christian women, using the apostle Paul as his spokesperson.

The Women of Paul's Letters

The apostle Paul recognized and had high regard for the women he encountered in his life and those within the Christian congregation. This he made very clear in his writings, expressing their value in the congregation and within the family. In his first letter to the Thessalonians, he compared the desirable qualities of a pastor to a nursing mother. – 1 Thessalonians 2:7.

When we take not of the many Christian women mentioned by name in his letters, he speaks warmly of them, commending them. When he closed his letters to the Christians in Rome, he specifically mentioned certain women "who has worked hard in the Lord." (Rom. 16:12) Concerning Euodia and Syntyche, he encouraged the brothers in Philippi to "help these women, who have struggled along with me in the gospel." (Phil. 4:3) In Paul's second letter to Timothy, Paul conveyed his appreciation for Lois and Eunice's exemplary faith, the grandmother and mother of Timothy. (2 Tim. 1:5) Then, we have the married couple Aquila and Prisca, who worked alongside Paul and had a close personal friendship with him. Both Aquila and his wife, Prisca, "risked their necks for my [Paul's] life." – Romans 16:3-4.

Did Paul Evidence Anti-female Bias?

1 Timothy 5:1-2 Updated American Standard Version (UASV)

5 Do not severely rebuke an older man, but rather appeal to him as a father, to the younger men as brothers, **2** older women as mothers, younger women as sisters, in all purity.

Here we can clearly see the apostle Paul's words to Timothy, the young man who was going to carry on in his place after Paul was martyred, reflect wholesome respect for women. Paul expressed an equal honor and concern for men and women within the Christian congregation. A verse that we have viewed before makes this all too clear. "There is neither Jew nor Greek, there is neither slave nor free man, there is neither male nor female; for you are all one in Christ Jesus." – Galatians 3:28.

Concerning the husband and the wife, Paul wrote: "Wives, be in subjection to your own husbands, as to the Lord. For the husband is the head of the wife, as Christ also is the head of the congregation, he himself being the Savior of the body." (Eph. 5:22, 23; compare 1 Cor. 11:3.) Yes, the husband and the wife's individual roles are different, but what would one expect. Moreover, this does not in any way imply that the wife is inferior. The husband and wife complement each other and the carrying out of God's will and purpose in this matter, not Paul's will, creates a challenge in the world that we live in today, but it helps family well-being if accomplished. Further, when the husband uses his headship, it is not to be oppressive, abusive, or unloving. Continued Paul: "husbands should love their wives as their own bodies" and be willing to make tremendous sacrifices for them. (Eph. 5:28-29) Children were to be obedient to both the father and the mother. – Ephesians 6:1-2.

We should also mention what the apostle Paul had to say about intimacy within the marriage. Applying to both the husband and the wife, Paul wrote: "The husband must fulfill his obligation to his wife, and likewise also the wife to her husband. 4 The wife does not have authority over her own body, but her husband does. And likewise, also the husband does not have authority over his own body, but his wife does." – 1 Corinthians 7:3-4.

"Woman ... to Be in Silence"

Woman (Gr., *gunē*), as it is used here in the singular, means women in general, not just wives,[37] as it has throughout this section of text (8-15). In verse 9, Paul addresses how women are to carry themselves, namely, their dress and outward appearance. In verse 10, Paul speaks of what is proper for women, who profess godliness, which is that they should be helpful to others; in other words, good works.

In silence (Gr., *hesuchia*) meant that the woman was 'to be quietness,' 'to be still.' In other words, she was to show respect for her head, man, especially the leadership of the congregation by not raising questions, attempting to teach.

---

[37] R. C. H. Lenski, The Interpretation of St. Paul's Epistles to the Colossians, to the Thessalonians, to Timothy, to Titus, and to Philemon (Columbus, Oh.: Wartburg, 1946), 562.

This was not a life of silence, just at the Christian congregation meetings. They were quietly to receive instruction at the meetings, and to ask their husbands questions in private, at home. Thus, in the public meeting, the woman was to learn by listening, not teaching through questions. – 1 Corinthians 14:34-35.

To the progressive modern-day mind, the words of 1 Timothy 2:12, Paul's statement that women are to "to be in silence," is a result from his antifemale bias. This simply is not the case. The "silence" mentioned here is in relation to the issue of teaching and spiritual authority in the context of the Christian congregation, which is out of the section for the Holy Spirit prescribed man-woman relationship.

William Hendriksen and Simon J. Kistemaker, *Exposition of the Pastoral Epistles,*

> **Let a woman learn in silence with complete submissiveness. But to teach I do not permit a woman, nor to exercise authority over a man, but to remain silent.**
>
> Though these words and their parallel in 1 Cor. 14:33–35 may sound a trifle unfriendly, in reality they are the very opposite. In fact, they are expressive of a feeling of tender sympathy and basic understanding. They mean: let a woman not enter a sphere of activity for which by dint of her very creation she is not suited. Let not a bird try to dwell under water. Let not a fish try to live on land. Let not a woman yearn to exercise authority over a man by lecturing him in public worship. For the sake both of herself and of the spiritual welfare of the church such unholy tampering with divine authority is forbidden.
>
> In the service of the Word on the day of the Lord a woman should *learn, not teach*. She should *be silent, remain calm* (see N.T.C. on 1 Thess. 4:11 and on 2 Thess. 3:12).

> She should *not cause her voice to be heard*. Moreover, this learning in silence should not be with a rebellious attitude of heart but "with complete *submissiveness*" (cf. 2 Cor. 9:13; Gal. 2:5; 1 Tim. 3:4). She should cheerfully *range herself under* God's law for her life. Her full spiritual equality with men as a sharer in all the blessings of salvation (Gal. 3:28: "there can be no male and female") does not imply any basic change in her nature *as woman* or in the corresponding task which she *as a woman* is called upon to perform. Let a woman remain a woman! Anything else Paul *cannot permit. Paul* cannot permit it because *God's holy law* does not permit it (1 Cor. 14:34). That holy law is his will as expressed in the Pentateuch, particularly in the story of woman's creation and of her fall (see especially Gen. 2:18–25; 3:16). Hence, *to teach*, that is, to preach in an official manner, and thus by means of the proclamation of the Word in public worship to *exercise authority* over a man, *to dominate him*, is wrong for a woman. She must not assume the role of a master.[38]

Let me try and qualify the last thought of Hendriksen and Kistemaker here. A woman cannot teach **God's Word** to a baptized born-again man in any official capacity: pastor, assistant pastor, deacon (servant). She cannot run a church Bible study class if it has men in that church Bible study class. She can teach women and children, as long as the male youth are not baptized born-again. She can participate in the church Bible study class by answering questions. The latter is not teaching in any official capacity. She can serve as a missionary. She can evangelize in the church community or any community for that matter because the men are

---

[38] William Hendriksen and Simon J. Kistemaker, *Exposition of the Pastoral Epistles*, vol. 4, New Testament Commentary (Grand Rapids: Baker Book House, 1953–2001), 108–109.

unbelievers. She can author Christian books. She can teach seminary or Bible college classes that are not directly related to training men for pastoral work. The home where the husband would take the lead in a family Bible study is an extension of the church. The seminary is also an extension of the church, where it would defy logic that a female professor would teach any course that are used to train pastors. If one cannot be a pastor, it only seems natural that the same person cannot train pastors. All other seminary courses are a grey area and are up to the Christian conscience of the female.

Full Submissiveness

Paul writes, "Let a woman learn in silence with **full submissiveness**." The direction given here from God by way of Paul has nothing to do with the woman surrendering her mind or her inner feeling or inner self that acts as a guide to the rightness or wrongness of her behavior or her ability to make decisions for herself. The phrase "with full submissiveness" is a divine warning against her seeking to usurp the position of authority within the Christian congregation, which is stated in the next verse.

This does not mean that women are not allowed to teach the Word of God to others. The apostle Paul encouraged "Older women … to teach what is good, and so train the young women." (Titus 2:3-5) Paul recalls two examples. "I am reminded of your sincere faith, a faith that dwelt first in your grandmother Lois and your mother Eunice, and now, I am sure, dwells in you as well." (2 Tim. 1:5) To reiterate, today, many Christian women who are obedient to God's Word teach Bible study classes to females or the youth within the Christian congregation. They can also evangelize outside of the church. Moreover, they can also be authors of Christian books, blogs, and so on. — Psalm 68:11; Matthew 28:19; Philippians 4:2, 3.

Thus, Paul's writings, viewed in their entirety, in no way justify the false accusation of antifemale bias.

CHAPTER 3 Gender-Inclusive Language in Bible Translation

The reader of Andrews' writings has continuously read interpretive and translation principles that are sound and aid the Christian in understanding the Bible more fully. One such interpretive principle is about the meaning that we are after, what the author meant by the words that he used as should have been understood by his initial intended audience.

When we look at the controversy over gender-inclusive language and the use of plurals, the above principles come into play, as does the historical-grammatical approach, which means that God personally chose the time, the place, the language, and the culture into which his Word was inspirationally penned. Who are we to disrespect that because we wish to appease the modern man or woman, who may be offended? Their offense is nothing more than self-centeredness, refusing to wrap their mind around the idea that the Creator of all things chose the setting, the language, and time in which his Word was to be introduced to man. One of the last bastions of literal translation philosophy, the New American Standard Bible, has given into the gender-inclusive translation philosophy. How are we to translate the Greek word ἀδελφοί (brothers)?

NEW AMERICAN STANDARD BIBLE (NASB 1995/2020): The 1995 edition **was*** very literal. The NASB Translates "brothers" or "brethren," to "brothers and sisters." The NASB has gender-inclusive changes to the word "man" in Romans 2:1-11 and Micah 6:8.

*The NASB 2020 revision has taken the first steps at abandoning their literal translation philosophy. One of the updates is what the NASB (the Lockman Foundation) calls the use of the "**Gender Accurate**" language. This is actually good marketing skills to call an abandonment of your core translation values "accurate" when it is anything but accurate.

1 Thessalonians 5:14: *We urge you,* **brethren***, admonish the unruly, encourage the fainthearted, help the weak, be patient with everyone.* NASB 1995

1 Thessalonians 5:14: *We urge you,* **brothers and sisters,** *admonish the unruly, encourage the fainthearted, help the weak, be patient with everyone.* NASB 2020

Romans 2:1: *Therefore you have no excuse,* **you foolish person***, everyone of you who passes judgment, for in that which you judge* **someone else** *[another], you condemn yourself; for you who judge practice the same things…*

Romans 2:3: *But do you suppose this,* **you foolish person** *[O man]* **who passes** *[when you pass] judgment on those who practice such things and* **yet does them as well** *[do the same yourself], that you will escape the judgment of God?*

Micah 6:8: *He has told you,* **O man***, what is good…* NASB 1995

Micah 6:8: *He has told you,* **a human***, what is good; and what does the LORD require of you but to do justice, to love kindness, and to walk humbly with your God?* NASB 2020

From what the Lockman Foundation has released about the upcoming 2020NASB, The 2020 update seems like it is going to be a more significant release than their 1995 update was. Taking everything into account, there are gender-neutral language changes. There is an attempt to remove archaic language which has also led to removing literal renderings, and that is not a good thing. We can say, some of the changes are good, some are irrelevant, some are wordy, and some are poor. Looking at all the pluses and minuses. There seem to be more minuses than pluses.

D. A. Carson in the publication: *The Challenge of Bible Translation* wishes to address the issue of gender-inclusive language and singular and plurals forms, in which he addresses comments made by Wayne A. Grudem and Vern S. Poythress. We will be addressing Carson's comments.

The Chief Translation Principle Is Accuracy

The chief principle that supersedes all others is accuracy, accuracy, and accuracy! In the above, we define Biblical meaning as the original author's intended meaning by the words he chose to use. Therefore, the translator accurately represents the exact wording and personal style of the original text and finds the corresponding English equivalent as far as the differences in grammar, syntax, and idiom will allow. In other words, he seeks 'to render the *words* of the original language text into an English equivalent (corresponding) word or phrase as *accurately* as possible.' The translator wants to re-express what the original language text says into an English equivalent, leaving it up to the reader to determine the meaning for himself. Therefore, it seeks to allow the reader to see the original text through the English equivalent.

Liberal-progressive Christianity has taken the driver's seat of the car of Christendom and has conservative Christianity riding in the back seat, if not the trunk. The liberal-progressive mindset is that homosexuality is only an acceptable alternative lifestyle. They believe that the Bible is nothing more than a book by man. That inspiration is not being led by "Holy Spirit," but being moved to pen something extraordinary, no different than a Shakespeare or even a John Grisham novel. Therefore, they accept the Bible as full of errors and that Adam and Eve are nothing more than allegorical (fictional) persons.

Making arguments such as 'the Bible authors wrote in a patriarchal time that influenced their writings, so to modernize the translation for the sake of those living in modern times causes no real harm, as this decreases the likelihood of offending the progressive, who might accept Christ.' The only problem with this argument is that you are rejecting inspiration of Scripture and full inerrancy of Scripture. What any Bible author wrote was under inspiration, which gives us God's thoughts, not men. Therefore, in essence, you are arguing that the Holy Spirit that moved the authors along to pen the thoughts of God was influenced by the patriarchal society of those time periods.

What these gender-inclusive translators fail to understand is this: to deviate, in any way, from the pattern, or likeness of how God brought his Word into existence, merely opens the Bible up to a book that reflects the age and time of its readers. Suppose we allow the Bible to be altered because the progressive woman's movement feels offended by masculine language. In that case, it will not be long before the Bible gives way to the homosexual communities being offended by God's Words in the epistle to the Romans. So, modern translations will then tame that language in an attempt not to offend. I am sure that we thought that we would never see the day of two men or two women being married by priests, but that day has been upon us for some time now. In fact, the American government is debating whether to change the definition of marriage. Therefore, I would suggest that the liberal readers do not take my warning here as radicalism, but more as reality.

Additionally: One has to consider the whole scope of translation issues. Let us look at the arguments directly from a modern thought-for-thought translation: Eugene Peterson:

> While I was teaching a class on Galatians, I began to realize that the adults in my class weren't feeling the vitality and directness that I sensed as I read and studied the New Testament in its original Greek. Writing straight from the original text, I began to attempt to bring into English the rhythms and idioms of the original language. I knew that the early readers of the New Testament were captured and engaged by these writings and I wanted my congregation to be impacted in the same way. I hoped to bring the New Testament to life for two different types of people: those who hadn't read the Bible because it seemed too distant and irrelevant and those who had read the Bible so much that it had become 'old hat.'

As we can see, the focus here is on the reader and trying to appease them, both new and old readers alike. Let us take a quick look at the words of the apostle Peter before commenting:

2 Peter 3:15-16 Updated American Standard Version (UASV)

¹⁵ and regard the patience of our Lord as salvation; just as also our beloved brother Paul, according to the wisdom given him, wrote to you, ¹⁶ as also in all his [the apostle Paul] letters, speaking in them of these things, in which are some things **hard to understand**, which the untaught and unstable distort, as they do also the rest of the Scriptures, to their own destruction.

The Bible is a very complex and profound book. There are many dozens of books available on how to interpret the Bible. Some of these books are over 600 pages long, with tiny print. To read these books, one has to have a dictionary in one hand and their hermeneutics book in the other. Do we not find it a bit ironic that one has to slow down and meditatively ponder through a book on understanding the Bible, yet we wish to put the Bible itself in sixth-seventh-grade language. Many of the words in these hermeneutic books are foreign to the lay reader: amanuensis, chiasm, exegesis, contextualization, criticism, didactic, etymology, genre, hermeneutics, *hyponoia*, metaphor, metonymy, pericope, perspicuity, proof-text, rhetoric, semantics, structuralism, synecdoche and so on. How many of these words do we think the new Bible reader knows offhand without going to a dictionary?

Herein is where the real problem lies. In the first century, all Christians were evangelizers. All Christians were obligated to be teachers of the good news, to make disciples. (Matthew 24:14, 28:19-20; Ac 1:8) Bible scholar John R. W. Stott noted:

Our failure to obey the implications of this command is the greatest weakness of evangelical Christians in the field of evangelism today. He added: We tend to proclaim our message from a distance. We sometimes appear like people who shout advice to drowning men from the safety of the seashore. We do not dive in to rescue them. We are afraid of getting wet.

Imagine this scenario: if every member of Christendom took on their responsibility to teach new persons, there would be no need to write a Bible translation at the sixth- grade level. Another factor to consider is, 'why are we so bent on adjusting God's Word to appease man that we neglect to be respectful of God's choice of when, how, and in what way his Word was to be made known?'

Hebrews 2:6 (English Standard Version)	**Hebrews 2:6** (Today's New International Version)
⁶ It has been testified somewhere, "What is man, that you are mindful of him? or the <u>son of man</u>, that you care for him?	⁶ But there is a place where someone has testified: "What are mere mortals that you are mindful of them, human beings that you care for them?
Psalm 8:4 (English Standard Version) [8:5 in the Hebrew text] ⁴ What is man, that you are mindful of him? and the son of man that you care for him?	**Psalm 8:4** (Today's New International Version) [8:5 in the Hebrew text] ⁴ what are mere mortals that you are mindful of *them*, human beings that you care for them?

In the Gospel accounts, the expression "son of man" is found over 80 times, with no scholar in denial that every instance applied to Jesus Christ, which is used by him to refer to himself. (Mt 8:20; 9:6; 10:23) There are several occurrences outside the Gospels, one being our above Hebrews 2:6.

The apostle Paul applied Psalm 8 as prophetic of Jesus Christ. In the book of Hebrews[39] (2:5-9), Paul quoted the verses, which read, "What is man [*enohsh*] that you are mindful of him, and the son of man [*benadham*] that you care of him? Yet you have made him a little lower than the heavenly beings ["angels" Septuagint; "a little lower than angels," at Hebrews 2:7] and crowned him with glory and honor. You have given him dominion over the works of your hands; you have put all things under his feet." (Ps 8:4-6; compare Ps 144:3, ESV) There is no doubt that Paul was applying this prophetic Psalm to Jesus, and stating that it

---

[39] https://christianpublishinghouse.co/2016/11/02/who-authored-the-book-of-hebrews-a-defense-for-pauline-authorship/

had been fulfilled in him, as Jesus was made "a little lower than angels," and becoming a mortal "son of man," in order that he may die and thereby "taste death for everyone." (Heb. 2:8-9) The TNIV has removed Christ from this prophecy at Psalm 8:4 and its application to him by Paul, with its mere mortals, them, human beings, and them. How do Carson and other gender-inclusive translators rationalize such a move? Carson writes:

In Psalm 8, the overwhelming majority of commentators see the expression as a **gentilic**, parallel to the Hebrew word for "man" in the preceding line. . . . In the context of the application of Psalm 8:4 to Jesus in Hebrews 2, one should at least recognize that the nature of the application to Jesus is disputed. Scanning my commentaries on Hebrews, over three-quarters of them do not think that "son of man" here functions as a messianic title but simply as a **gentilic**, as in Psalm 8.[11] If this exegesis is correct (and I shall argue elsewhere and at length that it is), Jesus is said to be "son of man," not in function of the messianic force of that title in Daniel 7:13-14, but in function of his becoming a human being – which all sides recognize is one of the major themes of Hebrews 2. (Scorgie, Strauss, & Voth, 2003, bolding mine)

The **gentilic criterion** requires one of two constructions: (1) It must end with, *hireq-yod* or (2) take the definite article.

Biblia Hebraica Stuttgartensia [Literal English Translation]

you remember him that and <u>son of man</u> you remember him that man what (is)

Take note that *ben-adam* of Genesis 8:4 fit neither of the gentilic criterions: (1) It must end with, *hireq-yod* or (2) take the definite article. In addition, Carson claims 'most commentators hold that it is not a messianic title, but apply it to the Messiah.' In response to that, we would suggest that we skip what most people think because much of mankind's tragedies had come in what people had thought to be the case, when, in fact, they were just plain wrong. Also, why block the reader from the possibility? Why not let the reader have the literal words, instead of a translator's interpretation of, and allow the reader to decide through their own exegesis, what the author of Hebrews meant by those words. Moreover, the writer of Hebrews would likely have been aware of Matthew's Gospel written in Hebrew and the Greek edition as well, in which "son of man" is used some 31 times. In addition, the readers of the book of Hebrews, the Jewish Christians, would be reading the Greek phrase *huios anthrōpou* ("son of man") in the Greek Septuagint at Psalm 8 as well. Moreover, by now the Gospels had been published **orally** for almost 30-years and Matthew in written form for about 15-years, making known that Jesus referred to himself as *huios anthrōpou* ("son of man"). If Jesus applied this title to himself, it should be evident that the writer of Hebrews was doing no less, and at least the original readers had a chance to reach this conclusion because the exact words were not hidden from them.

The TNIV and its plural "human beings" for *huios anthrōpou* ("son of man") go beyond translation and gets into playing the role of a commentary. First, we have the rendering of a singular as a plural. Second, "human beings" inappropriate though it may be is meant to convey the idea of humankind, but we have a word that is left out: *huios* (son) in the Greek of Hebrews 2:6 and *bēn* (son) in the Hebrew of Psalm 8:4. In this, we are losing the father-son relationship.

Those who speak and read English enjoy the benefit of having more than 100 different English translations. If one translation does not fit our preconceived notion of what a particular passage says, we can simply choose another and another until we find a translation that reads the way we want. If we search through the translations until we find the rendering of our choice; then, what have we learned that we already did not know? God's Word is a revelation from our Heavenly Father about himself, his will and purposes, to us, his creation. It was written in such a way, to …

(1) Help the reader draw closer to his Creator

(2) Comprehend the issues within creation

(3) Understand why we are here and how we are to achieve a good life while we are still within Satan's system of things

(4) Direction to help us achieve life in the new heavens and earth to come under Christ and his kingdom

We are to mold ourselves to God's Word, which will give us the opportunity at the best possible life now and a hope at everlasting life when this age of wickedness ends. How is that to be done if our translators are busy adjusting his Word to suit the modern reader. Instead we need be adjusting ourselves to fit His Word? God's Word was rendered to reflect his choosing of the time, the place, the language, and the culture? It seems that sales and the need to please man [or woman in this case] have taken on more significance than the accurate message of God's Word.

The Updated American Standard Version[40] will be one of the most faithful and accurate translations to date by Christian Publishing House. It will remain faithful to the

---

[40] https://www.uasvbible.org/

original and what the authors penned. We will not go beyond the translator's responsibility and delve into the field of the interpreter.— Translating Truth!

Our primary purpose is to give the Bible readers what God said by way of his human authors, not what a translator thinks God meant in its place.—Truth Matters!

Our primary goal is to be accurate and faithful to the original text. A word's meaning is the interpreter's responsibility (i.e., reader), not the translator's.— Translating Truth!

Christian Publishing House relies on the generosity of its users. Every donation, regardless of the amount 100 percent, goes toward helping us bring about the most accurate literal translation to date.

https://www.uasvbible.org/donation

CHAPTER 4 What Does Wifely Subjection Mean?

Ephesians 5:22 Updated American Standard Version (UASV)

²² Wives, be **in subjection to your own husbands**, as to the Lord. ²³ For **the husband is the head of the wife**, as Christ also is the head of the congregation,⁴¹

As we can see in the above, the Word of God clearly states at Ephesians 5:22, "Wives, be **in subjection to your own husbands**, as to the Lord." What does it mean to be in subjection? Must a wife slavishly submit to every demand from her husband, regardless? Can she never act on your own and make decisions without the help or advice of her husband? Can she never think for herself or believe differently from her husband?

In order to answer these questions, let us look at a Bible account of a woman, Abigail, who acted wisely when she went against her husband, Nabal. David was God's chosen king of Israel. The people of Israel and King David showed great kindness to Nabal. Yet, Nabal addressed them angrily and screamed at them when King David made a request. King David did not take this well; he was going to deal harshly with this Nabal. Abigail realized how she, her husband, and the whole household were in grave danger. She got King David to turn back from his anger. – 1 Samuel 25:2-35.

Abigail admitted to David that her husband was a worthless man. She then helped David and his men out with

---

⁴¹ Gr *ekklesia* ("assembly")

the provisions they had asked for, which Nabal had withheld. Now, under normal circumstances, a loving wife should never publicly say something demeaning about her husband. Was Abigail wrong in speaking poorly of her husband? No, in this instance, she was saving her life, the lives of those in the house, and the life of her worthless husband. There is nothing in God's Word, which shows outside of this one time; Abigail made it a practice to talking badly about others. The account is also clear that Nabal did not complain about how Abigail handled things. However, in this situation, Godly wisdom meant that she needed to act independently, deciding without her husband's help or advice. Lastly, the Bible praises Abigail for her actions. – 1 Samuel 25:3, 25, 32-33.

Discernment Needed

It is not a good thing for a wife to feel as though she is pressured to do anything unwise or contrary to God's Word, simply because she is in subjection to her husband. In addition, she should not be made to feel guilty for taking the initiative in some essential matter, as was true of Abigail, not to mention Sarah with Abraham, in the case of Hagar and Ishmael.–Genesis 21:11-12.

The wife being in subjection to her husband is not an absolute obligation that she must comply with everything her husband says. How do we determine the difference? When the right principles are at stake, she may choose to disagree with her husband. However, this is no license to reject everything he says because the wife is falling back on this Scriptural principle here (bypassing the husband out of willfulness, spite, or other wrong motives). It is similar to the license to drive. As a licensed driver, you obey all the traffic laws. The laws gave you while you are on the road. But if a child walks out in front of you, you would choose to swerve so as to miss the child, even if it meant breaking the traffic laws, like going into the other lane or driving up on the sidewalk. This freedom, liberty to ignore the traffic laws in such an incidence does not give you the right to start ignoring minor traffic laws as you see fit. Lastly, even on the occasions when you show initiative or choose to disagree with your husband, you still do so in a godly manner.

The Husband Who Ignores His Headship

Under the direction of God's Word, it is the wife's goal and spirit of subjection that she cooperates with her husband, supporting his decisions. This is not burdensome if her husband is a spiritually mature Christian. If he is not, it can be a challenge.

If the husband is spiritually immature, how can the wife deal with this? Until the husband rightly assumes his role as the head of the house, she can offer her insights as suggestions on how to benefit the family. She is steering the relationship and slowly letting him take over the driving as he becomes more skilled in his role as the husband. However, continually nagging the husband would not be in line with the wife's biblical subjection. (Prov. 21:19) However, if the husband's poor decision is putting the family in jeopardy in any way, she may choose to follow the course that keeps the family safe.

Then, there is the wife who is married to the unbeliever, which raises the wifely subjection to an even greater challenge. Nevertheless, she should remain in subjection as long as the Word of God is not being violated and the family is in no sort of jeopardy. If the husband does ask her to violate God's Law, she would "obey God rather than men."–Acts 5:29

Even wives and husbands who feel they have a good understanding of Scripture can overstep their role within the family at times. The husband may lack concern and thoughtfulness in his decision-making; the wife may press too hard to have her own way. How can they avoid this? It is by developing the quality of selflessness, where they do not put too much emphasis on self, as "we all stumble many times."—James 3:2.

Most men are very appreciative of a wife who shows initiative if it is done thoughtfully. Also, the level of cooperation is improved if both apologize when they make fall short due to human imperfection. We must remember how many times a day we sin against God, and he forgives us readily each time we ask. — Psalm 130:3-4.

CHAPTER 5 What Does Subjection in Marriage Mean?

The Christian woman that you marry will have to make many adjustments. The one that might affect her most will touch on her liberty. Before you married her, she was free to make the decisions about her life herself. She need not consult anyone if she did not want. Now that your wife is married, she is now obligated to consult you and get permission on major decisions that she formerly decided. Why is this so?

Because the Creator of humanity created man first, and then he created woman as the complement of the man. He assigned the man the role of the head of the wife and the future children. The feminist today "is a philosophy emphasizing the patriarchal roots of inequality between men and women, or, more specifically, social dominance of women by men. Radical feminism views patriarchy as dividing rights, privileges, and power primarily by gender, and as a result, oppressing women and privileging men."[42] This has caused a severe crisis in the God-ordained family arrangement of Christians. "Christian feminism is an aspect of feminist theology, which seeks to advance and understand the equality of men and women morally, socially, spiritually, and in leadership from a Christian perspective. Christian feminists argue that contributions by women in that direction are necessary for a complete

---

[42] Accessed August 28, 2019

https://www.thoughtco.com/what-is-radical-feminism-3528997

understanding of Christianity."[43] This is one reason for the high divorce rates among Christian families that we see today. In any organized group of people, from a nation to a family, someone has to have the final decision.

Ephesians 5:22 Updated American Standard Version (UASV)

22 Wives, be in subjection to your own husbands, as to the Lord.

The apostle Paul here and in verse 23 emphasizes subjection and respect. Yes, a wife is in subjection to her husband but this in no way means that she is inferior to her husband. Every living person in heaven and on earth is subject to someone. It is up to the husband to carry out his headship in a proper manner.

> **22** Within the marriage relationship wives[200] are addressed first, and they are urged to be subordinate to their[201] husbands as to the Lord. Although the verse does not contain any verb, 'submit' carries over from v. 21, with the imperative being understood instead of the participle.[202] The notion of submission in the preceding

---

[43] Harrison, Victoria S. "Modern Women, Traditional Abrahamic Religions and Interpreting Sacred Texts." *Feminist Theology: The Journal of the Britain & Ireland School of Feminist Theology* 15.2 (2007):145-159.

[200] Here the nominative case with the article (αἱ γυναῖκες), rather than the vocative, is used in address (cf. BDF §147[3]). It is 'wives' who are in view, not women generally.

[201] Although the adjective ἴδιος originally signified what was 'one's own', by New Testament times it differed little from a reflexive or possessive pronoun. In this context it is rendered '*their* husbands' (so BAGD, 369; Bruce, 384; Schnackenburg, 246; and Best, 532).

[202] The verb 'submit' does not appear in the best Greek text, so that the verse is dependent for its sense on the participle of v. 21. This is the reading of 𝔓[46] B Clement Origen and several Greek mss. according to Jerome. Other textual

verse is now unpacked without repeating the verb.[203] As we have already seen, the keyword rendered 'submit' has to do with the subordination of someone in an ordered array to another who is above the first, that is, in authority over that person. At the heart of this submission is the notion of 'order'. God has established certain leadership and authority roles within the family, and submission is a humble recognition of that divine ordering. The apostle is not urging every woman to submit to every man, but wives to their husbands. The use of the middle voice of this verb (cf. Col. 3:18) emphasizes the voluntary character of the submission. Paul's admonition to wives is an appeal to free and responsible persons which can only be heeded voluntarily, never by the elimination or breaking of the human will, much less by means of a servile submissiveness.[204]

The idea of subordination to authority in general, as well as in the family, is out of favour in a world which prizes permissiveness and freedom. Christians are often affected by these attitudes. Subordination smacks of exploitation and oppression that are deeply resented. But authority is not synonymous with tyranny, and the submission to which the apostle refers does not imply inferiority. Wives and husbands (as well as children and

---

traditions supply some form of ὑποτάσσειν ('submit') before or after τοῖς ἰδίοις ἀνδράσιν ('their husbands'), such as ὑποτάσσεσθε ('be subject') or ὑποτασσέσθωσαν ('let them be subject'). Most editors argue for the omission of the verb because it is the shorter reading and it is likely that later scribes included the verb for the sake of clarity. For a detailed discussion, see B. M. Metzger, *Textual Commentary*, 608–9.

[203] D. B. Wallace, *Greek Grammar*, 659.

[204] Cf. Barth, 609. M. J. Harris, *Colossians and Philemon* (Grand Rapids: Eerdmans, 1991), 178, comments: 'It is a case of voluntary submission in recognition of the God-appointed leadership of the husband and the divinely ordained hierarchical order in creation (cf. 1 Cor. 11:3–9)'.

parents, servants and masters) have different God-appointed roles, but all have equal dignity because they have been made in the divine image and in Christ have put on the new person who is created to be like God (4:24).[205] Having described the single new humanity which God is creating in his Son, with its focus on the oneness in Christ of all, especially Jew and Gentile (cf. Col. 3:11; Gal. 3:28), the apostle 'does not now [in this household table] destroy his own thesis by erecting new barriers of sex, age and rank in God's new society in which they have been abolished'.[206] That the verb 'submit, be subordinate' can be used of Christ's submission to the authority of the Father (1 Cor. 15:28) shows that it can denote a functional subordination without implying inferiority, or less honour and glory.[207]

The motivation for the wife to be subject to her husband is spelled out in the final phrase, *as to the Lord*.[208] The general admonition of v. 21 to be submissive in 'the fear of Christ' finds concrete expression for the wife in the marriage situation: as she is subordinate to her husband, so in that very action she is submitting to the Lord. Her voluntary response is not called for because of her role in society, nor is it to be understood as separate from her submission to Christ. Rather, it is part and parcel of the way that she serves the Lord Jesus (cf. Col. 3:23 of servants who engage in wholehearted work for

---

[205] 'Equality of *worth* is not identity of *role*', J. H. Yoder, cited by Stott, 218.

[206] Stott, 217. Note his timely discussion of v. 22 in the light of contemporary attitudes (215–20).

[207] Against the view of G. Bilezikian, 'Hermeneutical Bungee-Jumping: Subordination in the Godhead', *JETS* 40 (1997), 57–68.

[208] 'Lord' (κύριος) is not a reference to her husband, as some have claimed. The plural 'to their lords' (τοῖς κυρίοις) would have been written to correspond to 'to their husbands' (τοῖς ἰδίοις ἀνδράσιν).

> their masters and in that very action serve their heavenly Lord).[44]

Ephesians 5:23 Updated American Standard Version (UASV)

[23] For **the husband is the head of the wife**, as Christ also is the head of the congregation,[45] he himself being the Savior of the body.

Again, this verse is not a license to abuse or dominate the wife. It does mean that the husband has the final say in everything as long as he does not require the wife to break God's law. However, only the foolish husband would not consider the insights of his wife. When she is correct, humbly accept her direction. A husband may feel that headship permits him to absolute control. However, this is not so. His wife, though in subjection, is not his slave. She is a complement. (Gen. 2:18)

> **23** The reason for the wife's submission to her husband is now expressed through the causal clause: 'for the husband is head of the wife as Christ also is head of the church'. On two earlier occasions in Ephesians the key term 'head' has been used, both with reference to Christ (1:22; 4:15). Now, for the first time, the husband's headship is stated as a fact, and made the basis of his wife's submission. The origin of this headship is not elaborated here, although in the fuller treatments of 1 Corinthians 11:3–12 and 1 Timothy 2:11–13 it is

---

[44] Peter Thomas O'Brien, *The Letter to the Ephesians*, The Pillar New Testament Commentary (Grand Rapids, MI: W.B. Eerdmans Publishing Co., 1999), 411–412.

[45] Gr *ekklesia* ("assembly")

grounded in the order of creation, especially the narrative of Genesis 2 (cf. 1 Cor. 11:8, 9).

In each of the earlier instances of this term in Ephesians it signifies 'head' as 'ruler' or 'authority',[209] rather than 'source',[210] or one who is 'prominent, preeminent'.[211] At 1:22 'head' expresses the idea of Christ's supremacy and authority over the cosmos, especially the evil powers, which he exercises on behalf of the church (cf. Col. 1:18; 2:10). His rule over his people is described at 4:15, and this headship is expressed in his care and nourishment, as well as in his leadership of them in the fulfilment of the divine purposes.[212] Here the headship of the husband, in the light of the usage at 1:22,

---

[209] So W. Grudem, 'Does *kephalē* ('head') Mean "Source" or "Authority Over" in Greek Literature? A Survey of 2,336 Examples', *TrinJ* 6 (1985), 38–59; and 'The Meaning of Κεφαλή ('Head'): A Response to Recent Studies', *TrinJ* 11 (1990), 3–72. Note the summary of the debate by J. A. Fitzmyer, 'Kephale in 1 Corinthians 11:3', *Int* 47 (1993), 52–59; see also the detailed discussion of G. W. Dawes, *The Body*, 122–49, who concludes that κεφαλή is used as a metaphor indicating 'authority over'. Only in this verse in Ephesians, however, does the term have 'two distinct referents', namely, Christ and the husband.

[210] Advocates of the meaning 'source' include S. Bedale, 'The Meaning of κεφαλή in the Pauline Epistles', *JTS* 5 (1954), 211–15; G. D. Fee, *1 Corinthians*, 502–5; C. C. Kroeger, '*Head*', 267–83; and *DPL*, 375–77.

[211] A. Perriman, *Speaking of Women*, 13–33, who rejects both 'source, origin' and 'leadership, authority over' as meanings for κεφαλή, argues in favour of the term signifying 'prominence' or 'pre-eminence'. He acknowledges that this may 'also entail authority and leadership', but 'it is a mistake to include this as part of the common denotation of the term' (31; cf. Hoehner). This interpretation, however, runs into difficulties with the expression 'Christ is head of the church' (Paul is saying more than that Christ is pre-eminent in relation to the church, though this is true), while his exegesis of vv. 23–24 (55–57) is not convincing. The ἀλλά ('but') in v. 24 does not signify a change of emphasis from headship (v. 23), which only has to do with prominence and preeminence, to subordination with its notions of authority over others. Instead, the adversative ἀλλά ('but') provides a contrast with the preceding clause, 'he himself is the Saviour of the body' (v. 23c), which is not true of the husband's relationship to his wife (see on v. 24).

[212] C. E. Arnold, 'Jesus Christ', 365.

the general context of the authority structure of the Graeco-Roman household,[213] and the submission of the wife to her husband within marriage in vv. 22–24,[214] refers to his having authority over his wife; thus he is her leader or ruler.[215]

The mere presence of the terms 'head' and 'submission' in this context does not of itself 'establish stereotypes of masculine and feminine behaviour'.[216] Different cultures may assign different roles for men and women, husbands and wives. What is important here is that the nature of the husband's headship in God's new society is explained in relation to Christ's headship. The husband is head of the wife *as also*[217] Christ is head of the church. 'Although [Paul] ... grounds the fact of the husband's headship in creation, he defines it in relation to the headship of Christ the redeemer'.[218] Christ's

---

[213] For recent discussions of authority structures in the Graeco-Roman family see Lincoln, 357–59; and Hoehner.

[214] Cf. Lincoln, 369.

[215] Note the discussion of the lexical semantics of this, together with several criticisms of the view that 'head' means 'source', in P. Cotterell and M. Turner, *Linguistics and Biblical Interpretation* (London: SPCK, 1989), 141–45. They conclude that 'head' carries the sense of 'master' or 'lord'.

[216] Stott, 225.

[217] ὡς καί has comparative force, 'as also'. Cf. BAGD, 897; and Hoehner.

[218] Stott, 225. Contra Schnackenburg, 246, who acknowledges that Paul argues from creation in 1 Cor. 11, but considers this argument 'no longer convincing to us'. It loses its status in the light of Christ's headship, expressed in Eph. 5:23b. But if we assume that the 'author' of Ephesians is reflecting a view similar to that expressed in 1 Cor. 11, why should the words 'as Christ is head of the church' overthrow the husband's headship? It is better to speak of the latter being defined or explicated in the light of Christ's headship. K. H. Fleckenstein, *Ordnet euch einander unter in der Furcht Christi: Die Eheperikope in Eph 5, 21–33: Geschichte der Interpretation, Analyse und Aktualisierung des Textes* (Würzburg: Echter, 1994), 216, understands the role of the husband as 'head of the wife' to be derived from 'the patriarchal structure of the ancient family', but does not tie it to creation.

headship over the church is expressed by his loving it and giving his life for it, as vv. 25–27 so clearly show. This will have profound implications for the husband's behaviour as head of his wife (v. 28).

The additional words, 'he himself is the Saviour of the body', at first sight appear rather surprising and have caused exegetes to question whether they refer to the husband's role as his wife's protector or are part of the Christ-church/husband-wife analogy, thereby signifying that as Christ is the Saviour of the body, so also the husband is in some sense the saviour of his wife. While the term 'saviour' could possibly be taken in a general sense of protector or provider of the wife's welfare, so that the analogy of Christ's relationship to the church can be parallelled in the husband's 'saving' his wife, both syntax and usage are against it.

Instead, the clause is specifically focussed on Christ, not the husband: the personal pronoun 'he *himself*' is emphatic by its presence and position, and clearly refers to Christ. Nowhere in the context is the wife regarded as the husband's body as the church is Christ's body.[219] Further, the term 'saviour', which turns up twenty-four times in the New Testament, always refers to Jesus or God, but never to human beings.[220]

To interpret the words, then, of Christ[221] fits appropriately within the flow of the apostle's argument.

---

[219] The husband and the wife are 'one flesh' (5:31), and husbands are to love their wives 'as their own bodies', but this is a reference to the husbands' bodies, not the wives'.

[220] Of Jesus: Luke 2:11; John 4:42; Acts 5:31; 13:23; Phil. 3:20; 2 Tim. 1:10, etc. Of God: Luke 1:47; 1 Tim. 1:1; 2:3; 4:10, etc.

[221] The suggestions that 1 Cor. 7:16 (with its reference to the believing spouse being the instrument of the unbelieving spouse's salvation) and Tobit 6:18 (where Tobias marries his cousin Sarah to save her) provide significant parallels to

> Paul has been urging wives to be submissive to their husbands. The reason for this turns on the headship of the husband, which is parallel to Christ's headship or rule over the church. Paul then adds that the person who is head of the church is none other than the one who is the Saviour of the body. His saving activity, especially his sacrificial death (2:14–18; cf. 5:2), was for the deliverance of men and women in dire spiritual peril (2:1–10).
>
> Later in the paragraph, the apostle will urge husbands as heads of their wives to serve them in love. Their pattern is the Lord Jesus, whose headship was demonstrated in his loving the church and giving himself up for it, in order to present it faultless to himself (vv. 25–27).[46]

Subjection Is Relative

The husband's authority over his wife is not absolute; it is relative. We can consider the wife's subjection to the husband as a Christian is subject to the superior governing authorities. The apostle Paul said, "Let every soul[47] be in subjection to the governing authorities. For there is no authority except by God, and those that exist have been placed[48] by God." (Rom. 13:1) Yet, as Christian, while we obey the laws of the land, it is in conjunction with the Word of God. If any governmental authority asked us to do

---

the husband being the saviour of his wife have been shown to be unconvincing by Lincoln, 370, and Hoehner. Note the discussion in G. W. Dawes, *The Body*, 150.

[46] Peter Thomas O'Brien, *The Letter to the Ephesians*, The Pillar New Testament Commentary (Grand Rapids, MI: W.B. Eerdmans Publishing Co., 1999), 412–415.

[47] Or *person*

[48] Or *established, instituted*

something that breaks God's law, we obey what Peter and the apostles said, "We must obey God rather than men." (Ac 5:29) In a similar way, the wife is in subjection to her husband unless he is asking something of her that is against the Word of God.

1 Peter 3:1-2 Updated American Standard Version (UASV)

3 In the same way, you wives, be submissive to your own husbands so that even if any of them are disobedient to the word, they may be won without a word by the behavior of their wives, ² as they observe your chaste and respectful behavior.

3:1. These words are addressed generally to all Christian wives, but with special attention to those women whose husbands are not believers in Jesus Christ. **In the same way** takes the reader back to something previously introduced. The manner of behavior is described with the words, **be submissive to your husbands.** Submission appeared first in 2:13 in reference to the believer's response to authority and again in verse 18 in discussing the slave's response to the master.

Opinions vary widely as to how these injunctions should be defined. One well-intentioned but misguided commentator says that "the meaning of the wife's submission to her husband concerns the sexual relationship and should not be taken in a more general and oppressive sense" (Hillyer, 92). Such an interpretation not only violates the meaning of the word but also violates the context of this verse. Submission is best understood as "to voluntarily yield your rights or will to someone else's wishes or advice, as an expression of love for that person." Another spin on the term would be to define it as simply considering the needs of your husband and fulfilling them (Marshall, 99).

In all discussions related to submission, if the wishes, desires, or needs of the husband involve a direct violation of the Word of God, then submission does not apply. In such cases, to practice submission would involve violating the higher principle of obedience to God and his Word previously held out as the believer's goal (see 1:14–15, 22; 2:11).

Submitting oneself to another is the opposite of self-assertion, the opposite of an independent, autocratic spirit. It is the desire to get along with someone else. It involves being satisfied at times with less than what one may deserve or claim as a right. The goal of this type of behavior is to win over to Christ the non-believing husband. This occurs **without words.** This does not mean that a wife is never to speak, but rather that she is not to resort to constant arguments and nagging discussions. The husband will be more influenced by **the behavior** of his wife. This links this chapter to chapter 2, where verse 12 indicates that the non-Christian audience can be positively influenced for Christ as they observe the consistent and godly behavior of a believer.

As Christian wives live out the declaration of the praises of God, their husbands will be influenced. For the Christian wife living with a non-Christian husband, Peter's previous discussion of suffering even while doing what is right may have some application even within the context of her marriage and home. What a Christian wife says often will not change her husband; how she lives out her faith before him will make the difference.

3:2. Living a life of **purity and reverence** can make a difference. Purity signifies more than just moral or sexual purity, although this is included. The term suggests moral and ethical behavior that maintains a high standard. According to recent surveys, forty percent of the women polled by *USA Today* indicated that they have had extramarital affairs. Obviously, Peter's advice is still relevant today. Purity of life will generally not occur, however, unless "reverence" is also a part of it. The "reverence" is for the Lord and indicates a deep desire to keep his commandments. This desire to obey God

> should be the driving motive, resulting in a high moral standard.[49]

Ephesians 5:24 Updated American Standard Version (UASV)

24 But as the congregation[50] is subject to Christ, so also the wives should be to their husbands in everything.

> **24** The church's submission to Christ is now presented as the model of the wife's submission to her husband. The exhortation to wives in v. 22 is repeated and reinforced with the addition of the words 'in everything'. Here, however, the sequence of v. 22 is reversed. The analogy of the church being subject to Christ is mentioned before the admonition that *wives should submit to their husbands in everything.*
>
> Although the NIV's introductory *now* does not indicate it, the verse begins with the adversative conjunction 'but', which provides a contrast with the preceding clause, 'he himself is the Saviour of the body' (v. 23c).[222] This is not true of the husband's relationship

---

[49] David Walls and Max Anders, *I & II Peter, I, II & III John, Jude*, vol. 11, Holman New Testament Commentary (Nashville, TN: Broadman & Holman Publishers, 1999), 48–49.

[50] Gr *ekklesia* ("assembly")

NIV New International Version

[222] So the majority of commentators, including Calvin, Alford, Meyer, Abbott, M. Barth, Sampley, Schnackenburg, Lincoln, and Hoehner. This is better than regarding the ἀλλά as having resumptive ('consequently'; so Robinson, 124, 205; and Bruce, 385) or consecutive force (S. F. Miletic, *"One Flesh": Eph. 5.22–24, 5.31: Marriage and the New Creation* [Rome: Pontifical Biblical Institute, 1988], 102–3). The variations in the English versions ('therefore': AV; 'but': RV, ASV, NASB, NEB; 'and': TEV, JB, NJB; 'now': NIV; or the conjunction was left untranslated: RSV, NRSV) indicate something of the difficulties translators have had in understanding the force of the conjunction (so Hoehner).

to his wife. Although he has responsibility for her welfare, he is not her saviour (see on v. 23). So by means of the adversative 'but' (= 'notwithstanding this difference')[223] Paul makes the distinction between Christ and the husband, before comparing the church's submission to Christ with the wife's submission to her husband.[224] By using the same verb 'submit' (a middle voice in the original) the apostle stresses the willing character of the church's submission to Christ, and thus underscores what has already been asserted in v. 22 about the free and voluntary nature of the wife's subordination to her husband.

But what is involved in the church's submission to Christ, and what light does this throw on the wife's submission to her husband? The church's relationship to Christ is the focus of attention in several passages within Ephesians, and these spell out important facets of its submission to its Lord. God has graciously placed everything under Christ's feet and caused him to be head over all for the benefit of the church. The church gladly submits to his beneficent rule (1:22). Christ is the vital cornerstone on whom God's building is constructed. As this new community looks to Christ it grows and progresses to its ultimate goal of holiness (2:20, 21). Christ indwells the hearts of his people, establishing them so that they may be able to comprehend the greatness of his love (3:17, 19). The church receives Christ's gift of grace (4:7), and the ministers he gives for the purpose of

---

[223] Cf. Abbott, 166.

[224] The comparative particle ὡς ('as') begins the comparison, and this is balanced by the adverbial particle οὕτως ('so') and the conjunction καί ('and') which introduce the second clause. Wives (αὐ γυναῖκες) are the subject of the admonition, and the present middle imperative ὑποτασσέσθωσαν ('let them be subordinate') needs to be supplied (A. T. Robertson, *Greek Grammar*, 394).

enriching the whole body (4:11, 12). The church thus grows towards its head, the ultimate goal of which is the whole measure of Christ's fulness (v. 13), and it receives from him all that is necessary for this growth (vv. 15, 16). In submitting to its Lord, God's people had 'learned Christ': they welcomed him as a living person and were shaped by his teaching (v. 20). This involved submitting to his rule of righteousness and living by standards and values completely different from what they had known. The church is to imitate Christ's sacrificial love (5:2). It seeks to please its Lord (5:10) by living in goodness, holiness, and truth and by understanding his will (5:17). His people sing praises to him (5:19), and live in godly fear and awe of him (5:21). Accordingly, the church's submission to Christ means 'looking to its head for his beneficial rule, living by his norms, experiencing his presence and love, receiving from him gifts that will enable growth to maturity, and responding to him in gratitude and awe'.[225] It is these attitudes that the wife is urged to develop as she submits to her husband.

The additional element which reinforces this exhortation (cf. v. 22) is the concluding phrase, 'in everything'. In the Colossians household table the similar expression 'in everything' is used of the *obedience* of children to parents (Col. 3:20), and of slaves to masters (Col. 3:22; cf. Tit. 3:9). Although this phrase has raised modern questions about the *limitations* of a wife's submission to her husband (arising out of the contemporary desire to control the scope of someone's authority, specifying what decisions a person in authority

---

[225] Lincoln, 372. Cf. S. F. Miletic, *"One Flesh"*, 43, who aptly comments that 'the Christ/church relationship provides direction ("to the Lord"), perception (husband as "head" as Christ is "head") and example (church as paradigm) for the wife's act of subordination'.

can make),[226] 'in everything' indicates that the wife is to be subordinate to her husband *in every area of life*. In this sense it is all-encompassing, and is not, as some have suggested, restricted to sexual matters or some other special sphere of their relationship. 'No part of her life should be outside of her relationship to her husband and outside of subordination to him'.[227] Just as the church is to submit to Christ in everything, so in every sphere wives are expected to submit to their husbands. The motivation for doing this is a true and godly reverence for Christ (5:21; cf. v. 33).

Furthermore, the exhortation to be subordinate 'in everything' should be read within the flow of the argument in the chapter. By God's design husband and wife are 'one flesh' (v. 31; Gen. 2:24), and the divine intention is that they should 'function together under one head, not as two autonomous individuals living together'.[228] This subordination of wife to husband 'has a practical aspect in that it creates a greater effectiveness in their working together as one'.[229] And it anticipates God's ultimate intention of bringing back all things into unity in Christ (1:10; see below).

The question, then, as to whether the wife is to submit to her husband regardless of what he commands

---

[226] Rightly noted by S. B. Clark, *Man and Woman*, 83.

[227] S. B. Clark, *Man and Woman*, 83. If 'in everything' refers to every sphere of the husband-wife relationship, then it confuses the issue to speak of 'complete obedience' or 'full and complete subordination' (as Lincoln, 373, does).

[228] G. W. Knight, 'Husbands and Wives as Analogues of Christ and the Church: Ephesians 5:21–33 and Colossians 3:18–19', in *Recovering Biblical Manhood and Womanhood: A Response to Evangelical Feminism*, ed. J. Piper and W. Grudem (Wheaton, IL: Crossway, 1991), 170. He adds that the wife's 'submission is coextensive with all aspects of their relationship'.

[229] S. B. Clark, *Man and Woman*, 81.

is not addressed. But the words 'in everything', however they are interpreted, are not intended to reverse the instructions and exhortations already laid upon *all* believers in the paraenesis of Ephesians 4–6. This admonition to wives in the household table cannot be interpreted as a kind of grid through which all the earlier exhortations are filtered in the interests of serving the husband's authority.[230] Further, it goes without saying that wives are not to be subordinate in matters that are sinful or contrary to God's commands (cf. Acts 5:29).

There is no suggestion that this exhortation to be submissive is intended to stifle the wife's thinking or acting. She should not act unilaterally, but rather submit willingly to her husband's leadership. 'Just as the church should willingly submit to Christ in all things and, if it does so, will not find that stifling, demeaning, or stultifying of growth and freedom, so also wives should willingly submit to their husbands in all things and, if they do so, will not find that stifling, demeaning, or stultifying'.[231] As with the other admonitions in the household table, God sets forth these instructions for our good.

Accordingly, the wife's submission to her husband is *not conditional* on his loving her after the pattern of Christ's love or showing his unceasing care for her. Later the apostle will make it clear that husbands are not to rule their wives insensitively (vv. 25–27). Those in authority should not 'lord it over' those who are led (2 Cor. 1:24).

---

[230] Barth, 620–21, points out that 'in everything' cannot mean mere blind obedience, especially when it would mean acting contrary to God's commands. On the other hand, it is inappropriate to 'compil[e] a short or long list of exemptions to prove that "in everything" actually means "not in everything"' (621)!

[231] G. W. Knight, 'Husbands and Wives', 170.

But the wife's response of submission, which is not an unthinking obedience to his leadership, is to be rendered gladly, irrespective of whether the husband will heed the injunctions explicitly addressed to him or not. Contrary to much contemporary Western thinking, there is no suggestion that wives are to be submissive to their husbands only if their husbands are loving. We have already seen that the church's submission to Christ leads to blessing, growth, and unity for God's people. Similarly, the wife's submission to her husband, as she seeks to honour the Lord Jesus Christ, will *ultimately* lead to divine blessing for herself and others.[51]

THE BASIS OF LOVE

Ephesians 5:22–33

Sometimes, the emphasis of this passage is entirely misplaced, and it is read as if its essence was the subordination of wife to husband. The single phrase, 'The husband is the head of the wife', is quoted in isolation. But the basis of the passage is not control; it is love. Paul says certain things about the love that a husband must have for his wife.

(1) It must be a *sacrificial* love. He must love her as Christ loved the Church and gave himself for the Church. It must never be a selfish love. Christ loved the Church, not that the Church might do things for him, but that he might do things for the Church. The fourth-century Church father John Chrysostom has a wonderful

---

[51] Peter Thomas O'Brien, *The Letter to the Ephesians*, The Pillar New Testament Commentary (Grand Rapids, MI: W.B. Eerdmans Publishing Co., 1999), 415–418.

expansion of this passage: 'Hast thou seen the measure of obedience? Hear also the measure of love. Wouldst thou that thy wife shouldst obey thee as the Church doth Christ? Have care thyself for her as Christ for the Church. And if it be needful that thou shouldst give thy life for her, or be cut to pieces a thousand times, or endure anything whatever, refuse it not … He brought the Church to his feet by his great care, not by threats nor fear nor any such thing; so do thou conduct thyself towards thy wife.'

The husband is head of the wife—true, Paul said that; but he also said that the husband must love the wife as Christ loved the Church, with a love which never exercises a tyranny of control but which is ready to make any sacrifice for her good.

(2) It must be a *purifying* love. Christ cleansed and consecrated the Church by the washing with water on the day when each member of the Church made a personal confession of faith. It may well be that Paul has in mind a Greek custom. One of the Greek marriage customs was that, before the bride was taken to her marriage, she was bathed in the water of a stream sacred to some god or goddess. In Athens, for instance, the bride was bathed in the waters of the Callirhoe, which was sacred to the goddess Athene. It is of baptism that Paul is thinking. By the washing of baptism and by the confession of faith, Christ sought to make for himself a Church, cleansed and consecrated, until there was neither soiling spot nor disfiguring wrinkle upon it. Any love which drags a person down is false. Any love which coarsens instead of refining the character, which necessitates deceit, which weakens the moral strength, is not love. Real love is the great purifier of life.

> (3) It must be a *caring* love. A man must love his wife as he loves his own body. Real love loves not to extract service, nor to ensure that its own physical comfort is attended to; it cherishes the one it loves. There is something very wrong when a man regards his wife, consciously or unconsciously, as simply the one who cooks his meals and washes his clothes and cleans his house and brings up his children.
>
> (4) It is an *unbreakable* love. For the sake of this love, a man leaves father and mother and is joined to his wife. They become one flesh. He is as united to her as the members of the body are united to each other, and would no more think of separating from her than of tearing his own body apart. Here indeed was an ideal in an age when men and women changed partners with as little thought as they changed clothes.
>
> (5) The whole relationship is *in the Lord*. In the Christian home, Jesus is an always-remembered, though an unseen, guest. In Christian marriage, there are not two partners, but three—and the third is Christ.[52]

The wife should feel and know that the husband is primarily concerned with her best interest and will always consider her views, evidencing that he values her voice in all matters. He will make sure that he listens to her, and if her view is the correct view, he will wisely follow that course. A husband will demonstrate and express his love and respect for his wife when he carries out his Godly assigned position as the head of the family. (John 13:34) The husband might be imperfect and fallible, but if he follows in the example of

---

[52] William Barclay, *The Letters to the Galatians and Ephesians*, The New Daily Study Bible (Louisville, KY; London: Westminster John Knox Press, 2002), 200–201.

Jesus Christ, he will have a wife that loves and respects him as well.

Other Book by Andrews

40 DAYS DEVOTIONAL FOR YOUTHS

COMING-OF-AGE IN CHRIST

Edward D. Andrews

HUSBANDS LOVE YOUR WIVES AS CHRIST
LOVED THE CHURCH. WIVES RESPECT YOUR
HUSBANDS. - EPHESIANS 5:25, 33

WRITTEN FOR HUSBANDS & WIVES

THE BIBLICAL MARRIAGE

BIBLICAL COUNSEL THAT WILL STRENGTHEN A
STRONG MARRIAGE AND SAVE A FAILING MARRIAGE

EDWARD D. ANDREWS

Bibliography

Andreas, K. J., Thomas, S. R., Burk, D., Yarbrough, B., & Butterfield, R. (2016). *WOMEN IN THE CHURCH: An Interpretation and Application of 1 Timothy 2:9-15*. Wheaton, IL: Crossway Books.

Arnold, C. E. (2002). *Zondervan Illustrated Bible Backgrounds Commentary Volume 3: Romans to Philemon*. Grand Rapids: Zondervan.

Bradley, A. B. (2010). *Liberating Black Theology: The Bible and the Black Experience in America*. Wheaton: Crossway.

Bucher, C. (Spring 2015). New Directions in Biblical Interpretation Revisited . *Bretheren Life and Thought 60, no. 1*, 36.

Daly, M. (1973). *Beyond God the Father: Toward a Philosophy of Liberation*. Boston: Beacon Press.

Geisler, N. L., & Nix, W. E. (1996). *A General Introduction to the Bible*. Chicago: Moody Press.

Grenz, S. J., & Olsen, R. E. (1992). *20th Century Theology: God & the World in a Transitional Age*. Downers Gove, IL: Intervarsity Press.

Hendriksen, W., & Kistemaker, S. J. (1953-2001). *Exposition of the Pastoral Epistles, New Testament Commentary vol. 4,*. Grand Rapid: Baker Book House.

Howe, T. A. (2015). *Objectivity in Biblical Interpretation*. Seattle: CreateSpace.

Kenneth L. Boles, Galatians & Ephesians, The College Press NIV Commentary. (1993). Joplin, MO: College Press.

Kimel Jr., A. F. (2001). *This Is My Name Forever: The Trinity & Gender Language for God.* Downers Grove: InterVarsity Press.

Knight, G. W. (1992). *The Pastoral Epistles: A Commentary on the Greek Text, New International Greek Testament Commentary.* Grand Rapids, MI; Carlisle, England:: W.B. Eerdmans; Paternoster Press, .

Larson, K. (2000). *Holman New Testament Commentary, vol. 9, I & II Thessalonians, I & II Timothy, Titus, Philemon.* Nashville, TN: Broadman & Holman Publishers.

Lenski, R. C. (1946). *The Interpretation of St. Paul's Epistles to the Colossians, to the Thessalonians, to Timothy, to Titus, and to Philemon.* Columbus, OH: Wartburg.

Reuther, R. R. (1983). *Sexism and God-Talk: Toward a Feminist Theology.* Boston: Beacon Press.

Ruether, R. R. (1986). *Women-Church: Theology and Practice of Feminist Liturgical Communities.* San Francisco: Harper and Row.

Russel, L. M. (1985). *Feminist Interpretation of the Bible.* Philadelphia: Westiminster.

Russell, L. M. (1985). *Feminist Interpretation of the Bible.* Philadelphia: Westminster Press.

Scorgie, G. G., Strauss, M. L., & Voth, S. M. (2003). *The Challenge of Bible Translation.* Grand Rapids: Zondervan.

Stanton, E. C. (1993). *The Women's Bible.* Boston: Northeastern University Press.

Tremper, L. I. (2005). *How to Read Genesis (How to Read Series How to Read).* Grand Rapids: Intervarsity Press.

Wainwright, W. J. (2005). *The Oxford Handbook of Philosophy of Religion*. New York: Oxford University.

Wallace, D. B. (1999). *Greek Grammar Beyond the Basics – Exegetical Syntax of the New Testament*. Grand Rapids, MI: Zondervan Publishing House.

Wheelock, F. M., & Lafleur, R. A. (2001). *Wheelock's Latin, 7th ed.* New York: Harper Collins.

Woodhead, L. (April 1997). Spiritualising the Sacred: A Critique of Feminist Theology. *Modern Theology 13, no.2*, 197.

Young, P. D. (1990). *Feminist Theology/Christian Theology: In Search of Method*. Eugene, OR: Wipf and Stock.

www.ingramcontent.com/pod-product-compliance
Lightning Source LLC
Chambersburg PA
CBHW060203050426
42446CB00013B/2963